Life Beyond IT

JOANNE BRADBURY DUSTIN

LIFE BEYOND IT

OPEN THE DOOR...YOUR FUTURE IS WAITING

2007

Life Beyond IT

TABLE OF CONTENTS

To All Of You Who Have So Graciously Shared Your Stories
To All Former Keane Consultants And Keane's Dedicated And
Caring HR Staff
To My Family: John, Jordan, Kim, Alex, And Michael MacNeill;
Jeanne, Kevin, Ryan, Megan And Michaela Killoran.
To My Good Friend And Editor: Betty Black
To My Mentor Coach, Marcia Bench

And Especially To My Partner And Best Friend, Robert Osborn.
Without Your Support And Encouragement, This Book Would
Never Have Been Written.

WHY I WROTE THIS BOOK

My intention in writing this book isn't lofty. It is, in fact, quite simple. I'd like to help those of you who are I.T. professionals identify and consider all of your career possibilities, both within and outside the world of I.T., so that you are well prepared for whatever the future may bring.

To enable this process, I have interviewed people who have left corporate I.T., either on their own or because of downsizing, outsourcing or offshoring. Each person told me his or her story, and I have tied the stories together through the themes of career development — knowing yourself, finding your passion and following it, realizing and enjoying your success.

Additionally, I too was an I.T. professional. I have over 25 years' experience in the industry in a variety of roles, from developer, to systems analyst, to project manager. Along the way, I discovered that what I enjoyed most about my work was enabling others to become masters of the processes and technology that are so essential to success in today's business organizations...so I moved from a purely I.T. role into the role of I.T. Training Manager, and then to broader roles that focused upon organizational change as well as employee development.

Throughout these years, there was constant change, both in I.T. and in the roles that I.T. professionals played. There were also major changes in the business environment that caused business leaders to pressure their I.T. organizations to "do more with less". And so the stage was set for the greatest change the American I.T. industry has ever experienced — outsourcing/offshoring thousands, some say millions, of I.T. jobs.

Before I launched my coaching and consulting practice, I was Director of Career Development for Keane, Inc., a well-established I.T. and management consulting firm based in Boston, Massachusetts, with over 10,000 employees in North America, the United Kingdom, India and Australia. I saw many highly-experienced, talented people in the U.S. lose their jobs. Why did this happen? Because the U.S. business environment was becoming more and more competitive and, for businesses to survive, their leaders believed they needed to drastically reduce their costs. The greatest expense in most businesses is salaries. When business leaders saw there was a potential pool of talent accessible at a fraction of the cost, they took advantage of it. Keane acquired a company with development centers in India and began moving work offshore. Recently, Keane was acquired by Caritor.

From the California International Business Report: Caritor Acquires Keane, Inc. for $854 Million, posted on February 12, 2007 by editor in India, Mergers and Acquisitions, Information Technology

"Caritor Inc, a $100 million California-headquartered global provider of IT services with a predominant presence in India, is acquiring US-based Keane Inc for $854 million in an all cash deal. Keane is a Boston headquartered publicly listed $900 million IT and BPO service provider. The combined entity will storm into the $1 billion league employing 14,000 employees...The new entity will have Keane as its name and the company will be taken private. The chairman of Caritor, Mani Subramanian, will be the Chairman and CEO of the new firm. Subramanian was among the key senior executives of Wipro during its growth days before leaving to start Caritor in 1993. The company was started as IT Solutions, which was then re-christened Caritor during 2004."

A VERY BRIEF HISTORY OF I.T.

Where have we been and where are we going?

In 500 B.C., the abacus was developed in China. The Chinese could not have foreseen the dramatic impact their invention would eventually have on the world!

Here's a list of other key events that paved the way for the I.T. profession we know today.

In 1642, Pascal invented the adding machine.

In 1822, Babbage created the first mechanical computer.

In 1896, The Tabulation Machine Company was founded, to become IBM in 1924.

In 1943, First Generation (vacuum tubes) computers

In 1957, the FORTRAN language

In 1959, Second Generation computers (magnetic core memory), along with the COBOL language

1964—Third Generation computers (integrated circuits)

1971—Fourth Generation computers (silicon chip microprocessors)

1975, Microsoft was founded

1976—Apple Computer was founded

1981—MS-DOS and PC-DOS

1985—Microsoft Windows

1991—Linux

1993—Intel Pentium and Windows NT

And most notably in the 1990's...

The Internet dramatically changed our world by drawing almost every U.S. household and many others, worldwide, into the realm of technology, paving the way for the post-millenium explosion of wireless technology.

Each of these advances in technology required professionals working with the technology to acquire new skill sets. As the pace of technological advances accelerated, it became more and more difficult for I.T. professionals to stay on top of these changes. But all business users of the technologies didn't adopt" the latest and greatest". For many businesses, these new technologies were cost-prohibitive. So, an extensive market for technical skills that were not "bleeding edge" developed.

Businesses developed their own large I.T. departments, competing for talent to maintain their extensive I.T. systems. Many U.S. computer professionals built their careers in that "short supply, high demand" market. And then the world changed. As the economies of the developing nations, such as India and China began to grow, they sought business opportunities beyond their geographic boundaries, especially opportunities in the United States. Because of developments in technology, they were able to leverage these opportunities by providing professional services "from a distance". Due to the economic differences between the U.S. and the developing nations, these I.T. professionals could provide the same services at a fraction of the cost of their U.S. counterparts. U.S. companies welcomed the opportunity to reduce their costs by taking advantage of this new business format that would become known to the world as "offshoring". The result was that many I.T. professionals who had built what they thought were comfortable careers were faced with heavy competition for the very jobs they had assumed would always be theirs. Unfortunately many of them lost their jobs as companies leapt onto the offshoring bandwagon.

I.T. professionals who found themselves in this predicament spent many months and sometimes even years searching for work. And when they found work, it was often at a reduced rate of pay. The result was the loss of more than only their jobs. Some lost their homes, their possessions, their life savings. Some lost their families through divorce. And, most tragically, some lost their lives. Here is one such story.

TNR Online, the Daily Express, Office Politics by Clay Risen

"For unemployed information-technology workers, the parking lot at Bank of America's Concord, California campus has become something akin to a holy shrine — not to mention the epicenter of an increasingly powerful labor movement. Recently scores of workers convened there for a day-long vigil, replete with candles. Their purpose? To commemorate Kevin Flanagan, a Bank of America software programmer who, just after getting laid off in April, walked out to his car and shot himself.

Flanagan, whose job was moved overseas to help cut costs, is far from the only IT expert to be priced out of work lately. Indeed, having already suffered through the seemingly interminable dot-com bust, tens of thousands of high-tech workers in Silicon Valley are now being threatened by offshore outsourcing, which is rapidly becoming an industry-altering trend. More than anything else, that fact explains how a mild-mannered, middle-aged techie became a martyr among some of the most educated workers in the country.

Conventional wisdom still holds that companies send their easiest, most mindless jobs to places like India, where cheap but literate labor can do work that most white-collar Americans would turn up their noses at. This may have been true five years ago, but today, virtually any job that doesn't require face-to-face-interaction is up for grabs

— programming, systems engineering, and even non-IT careers like financial analysis and accounting. The consulting firm Forrester Research predicts that in the next 12 years, 3.36 million white-collar service jobs will be "offshored," because companies in developing nations can do work at the same level of quality for a fraction of the cost..."

This article was published in 2003. The trend in I.T. spending in the U.S. has improved somewhat over the past several years. Offshoring is still prevalent, but many more U.S. I.T. jobs are available, and those I.T. professionals who felt they were mistreated by their employers during the economic downturn, recognizing that they now have a bit of an edge, are taking advantage of these opportunities. But the question is: How long will this trend continue?

In their article, The Next Job Boom, (Business 2.0 Magazine, May 3, 2006) Paul Kaihla, Erick Schonfeld and Paul Sloan say:

"How long will workers keep their current edge? It's impossible to know, and there are economic scenarios under which power could quickly revert back toward management. Another external shock on the order of 9/11, or, say, $100 per barrel of oil could swiftly put workers back at the mercy of their bosses.

Some economists also worry that, even absent such events, the U.S. economy could be headed into serious trouble because of towering fiscal and trade gaps, high consumer debt, a slowing housing market, and anemic overall wage growth. While examples of double-digit pops in salaries for skilled workers in tight labor markets abound, total wages for all workers have risen only slightly since the downturn. Taken together, all these factors lead some economists to believe that we may be headed for an unstable period of weakening consumer spending that derails the five-year-old recovery and ultimately stifles hiring"

While over the past several years a number of new I.T. jobs have been created, lessening the overall effect of offshoring, that trend is predicted to start slowing down once again soon (Expect a Tech Slowdown Before the Next Boom, Forrester Research's Long Term IT Spending Forecast — 2005–2010).

Don't you wish you had a crystal ball in which you could see the future?

GAZING INTO THE VIRTUAL CRYSTAL BALL

What does the future of I.T. look like?

In the Future of Software Conference 2007, the focus was "Back to Business": Enterprise Business Applications, Customer Relationship Management, Analytics and Business Intelligence, Middleware and SOA, Information and Data Management, Grid, Utility and Load Sharing.

Are any of these your areas of expertise? If so, you may be feeling pretty good about the future right now, thinking "Yes...my expertise fits," But...this is only one view.

Here's a different perspective of future areas of focus from Denise Dubie, Network World:

- Project management
- Information security
- Change management
- Vendor and sourcing management
- Interpersonal skills: communications; teamwork; systematic problem solving; planning, prioritizing and goal setting; decision making

And here's what Laura Schneider of Tech Careers says are the top 10 technical career skills (About.com):

1. Unix Operating System
2. Linux Operating System
3. Java Programming Language
4. C++ Programming Language
5. Perl Programming Language
6. MySQL Database Management
7. Microsoft C# Programming Language
8. XML — Extensible Markup Language
9. HTML Skills
10. Project Management Skills

Are you confused yet? Read on.

From Stacy Collett, Hot Skills, Cold Skills, Computerworld, July 17, 2006

"The most sought after corporate IT workers in 2010 may be those with no deep-seated technical skills at all. The nuts-and-bolts programming, and easy-to-document support jobs will have all gone to third-party providers in the U.S. or abroad. Instead, IT departments will be populated with "versatilists" — those with a technology background who also know the business sector inside and out, can architect and carry out IT plans that will add business value, and can cultivate relationships both inside and outside the company..."

And from Mary Brandel, Computerworld, May 24, 2007

"Those in search of eternal life need look no further than the computer industry. Here, last gasps are rarely taken, as aging systems crank away in back rooms across the U.S., not unlike 1970's reruns on Nickelodeon's TV Land. So while it may not be exactly easy for Novell NetWare engineers and OS/2 administrators to find employers who require their services, it's very difficult to declare these skills - or any computer skill, really - dead.

In fact, the harder you try to declare a technology dead, it seems, the more you turn up evidence of its continuing existence. Nevertheless, after speaking with several industry stalwarts, we've compiled a lost of skills and technologies that, while not dead, can perhaps be said to be in the process of dying. Or, as Stewart Padveen, Internet entrepreneur and currently founder of AdPickles, Inc., says "Obsolescence is a relative — not absolute — term in the world of technology".

1. COBOL
2. Nonrelational DBMS
3. Non-IP networks
4. Cc:Mail
5. ColdFusion
6. C programming
7. PowerBuilder
8. Certified Netware Engineers
9. PC network administrators
10. OS/2

Future Trends in I.T.

From "IBM, Intel and Microsoft Tout Technology Future" by Thomas Claburn, Information Week, 4/24/2007

"A glimpse into the future of computing technology, provided by researchers from IBM, Intel and Microsoft, reveals photo-realistic virtual worlds rendered on the fly, desktop file manipulation using hand gestures, and presence information relayed by ubiquitous sensors.

IBM is trying to understand the pain points in enterprises and provide the technology to help, i.e., providing presence information, knowing where people are and how best to interact with them at any given time — everyone in the future will be sensorized".

Summing it all up:

In the future, we know that technologies will proliferate, develop and change even more rapidly than today.

Do you enjoy learning new technologies, or enhancements to existing technologies, even without the benefit of training or even product manuals?

Rapid skills development will be a key differentiator in the future.

We know that old technologies do not often die suddenly but instead slowly fade away.

Do you have deep expertise in technologies for which it is already difficult to find skilled professional support?

We know that there will be more and more virtual project teams.

Do you enjoy working "virtually" — with little or no direct contact with your team?

Do you enjoy working across functions, cultures, geographies and generations?

Are you available to work 24X7?

Do you have strong "virtual team" program/project management skills?

Do you have strong subject matter expertise — technical skills and domain knowledge?

Teams will be formed "on the fly", composed of technicians with the right skills, available at the right time, for the right price. Most will be working as contractors or consultants. Are you resilient, flexible and adaptable?

If you're feeling like you may not fit well, what do you plan to do if you find yourself out of work in the future, with few or no opportunities?

Have you thought about looking for opportunities outside of I.T.? Or have you thought about becoming an independent I.T. consultant?

This book contains stories of people who left their corporate I.T. or I.T.-related jobs, either by choice or not, and found satisfaction in different careers. Several became independent consultants.

They're sharing their stories with you to help you consider what might be possible in your future. Please listen to their words of wisdom. By taking some time now to consider and create contingency plans, you can assure that you will thrive, no matter what the future may hold for you.

FOLLOW THE STRING

Upon first review of this book, my editor said, "These are very interesting stories, but there's something missing. They're like a string of pearls... without the string."

So I thought about the "string" — the common bond I had found that ties all of these stories together. And this presented me with a dilemma. Having worked with I.T. professionals for so many years, and having been one myself, I know that if what I'm conveying sounds at all "touchy feely" to you, I may lose your attention. So I'm asking you to please bear with me. The "string" connecting these stories is the story tellers' sense of purpose.

Each of us has a purpose in life. That doesn't mean there is someone out there who is determining what our purpose should be. It simply means that our lives matter; that we each make a difference in the world, and that difference is a reflection of our purpose.

One of the things I do with my coaching clients is to help them uncover their life purpose. You'll notice that I didn't say "discover". I say "uncover" because your purpose is already there, inside you, whether or not you recognize it right now.

This book is called "Life Beyond I.T.: Open the Door...Your Future is Waiting. On hearing this title, some people responded "Door? What door? What are you talking about?" The door I'm referring to is the barrier between you and those things you really want/need in your life. Uncovering and enacting your purpose is the key to unlocking the door.

Uncovering Your Life Purpose

Consider this: Have you ever been so enthralled with your activities that you've lost all sense of the passing of time? You've forgotten about watching your favorite TV show, and you've even forgotten to eat?

Some people refer to that as "being in the flow". Psychologist Mihaly Csikszcentmihalyi (pronounced mee-hi chick-zent-mee-hi) has studied and written about flow. According to Wikipedia, flow is so named because, during Csikszentmihalyi's interviews, several people described their experiences using the metaphor of "a current carrying them along". Csikszentmihalyi may have been the first to describe flow, however Eastern religions such Buddhism and Taoism have long recognized it. The phrase, "being at one with things" is a description of flow.

The concept of "being in the zone" during an athletic performance also describes the flow experience. The legendary soccer player, Pele, once said: I felt a strange calmness…a kind of euphoria. I felt I could run all day without tiring, that I could dribble through any of their team, or all of them…that I could almost pass through them physically. Wouldn't it be great if you were so fully engaged in your activities? What do you think your results would be?

Flow doesn't just happen. It comes from passion — from an emotional connection to your activities, from the feeling of loving what you're doing. And that love is grounded in a sense of purpose, a sense that the activities in which you're engaged have meaning and value.

Most people want their activities to be meaningful — they want to feel good about them. For example, someone might say, "I want to help save the world one person at a time, so I'm contributing a percentage of my earnings to Doctors Without Borders."

This statement is an expression of their sense of purpose. What's yours? Don't know? Maybe this will help. Your purpose doesn't have to be "lofty". It can be as simple as, "I work to provide a comfortable life for my family and to be an example to my children of how to be a successful person." The activities of someone who defines their purpose in this way might include acting as a soccer coach for her/his child's soccer league, or volunteering for school activities. A work-related activity might be "Proposing to the leadership team that a policy of flextime be implemented to afford parents the opportunity of participating in their children's school activities".

To be truly successful in your career and in your life, it's important that you do some soul-searching to find your own purpose and then align your career and life activities with it. Purpose provides both a foundation and framework for your career and your life. Uncovering your purpose unlocks the door to your future.

In my coaching practice, I assist my clients in developing their own life purpose statement. They fill in a worksheet I provide, they reflect on it, we talk about it, and as we continue through our coaching relationship, we revisit their life purpose, shaping and refining it, until it fits them so well that it becomes the driving force for their career and their personal lives. My mentor coach, Marcia Bench, MCCC (Master Certified Career Coach), helped me to define my life purpose and my career direction. This was, for me, a life-altering process. It is the foundation today of everything I am and everything I do. My life purpose is: to be all I can be by helping others to become all they can be through facilitating their self-understanding, growth and development. Marcia offers an excellent CD, Discovering Your Life Purpose, available on my website: www.careerlostandfound.com.

JUST DO IT!

Bob Zidle was a systems analyst and later a professional development manager in a high tech consulting company. He left his former role because the company was downsizing and the role changed drastically. It became more of a clerical function and also involved long-distance travel. It was no longer considered to be an essential function to the business, so it wasn't what he wanted to be doing. He says, "I didn't go through a period of depression as some do. People experience more of an impact when there is a surprise layoff. In my case it was a gradual situation and I was more prepared. I was ready to move on".

That was in September, 2003, and Bob spent a year after that deciding what he wanted to do with his career. Did he want another technical role? Did he want to consider entrepreneurship? He felt he was "sort of obsolete" for the technical environment. His strength was in mainframe and CICS. He had been able to convert his knowledge to website development but, he says, "There were kids coming out of grade school that knew more than I did. I had been out of the technical environment too long. I looked at it as the end of my technical career." Bob felt it was too soon to retire, so he looked for business opportunities in a way that didn't include high tech. He had other opportunities, and he was fortunate to be able to raise funds to develop a business.

About the decision process, Bob says that "It was about as shotgun an approach as it could have been!" First, he had a commercial realtor looking for driving ranges. The area he was looking in was well developed — not much opportunity to build a driving range. One spot was wetland — it didn't look wet, but showed up in the wetlands map. Others came about that were for sale — one he really liked — but before he got in the car it was sold! There was a broken down, weary one but it was priced as commercial land. He couldn't afford to buy it to build commercially. At that point he knew the driving range idea just wasn't going to happen. After three months, the shotgun approach really set in. Bob looked at a courier service, and then a laundromat/dry cleaner. This seemed like a great opportunity — $2,000 a week on the Laundromat side, $2,000 a week on the dry cleaning side. But then Bob sat with the proprietor for a week and she had only two customers! He realized that the money was a gross exaggeration and the proprietor was just looking to get out. He began to learn that "there are no pearls out there waiting to be purchased at a low price".

Bob knew he wanted to buy a business, but he also wanted to find a way for his wife, Jan, to retire. She had been in her job then for 17 years, and had originally only intended to work until the kids were out of college and the house was paid off. Bob's plan was to do something that would take some time to develop, maybe a year or two, and then would support both of them.

Another opportunity came along. It was a small motel, 15 rooms. The land wasn't going to appreciate significantly and there was no possibility of expanding. The local bank was "all too willing" to turn out half a million dollars. Bob and Jan would have had to sell their house and move into a smaller house near the motel. Summer would have been great but in winter it would have been somewhat isolated. Bob put in an offer, but after the first rejection, he just passed.

Next he looked at a courier service. Its primary business was transferring checks to processing centers. While negotiating the purchase, Bob did some internet research and discovered "the check clearing for the 21st century" act. There was a law enacted by congress that would be in place in the following year that would have made half the business obsolete. He lost some money in terms of due diligence, legal fees, etc. but he felt he was fortunate to escape.

During that time he was using the local shipping store for sending legal documents back and forth. He realized that this was a nice little business, so he looked into the possibility of a franchise. There were 5,000 of these stores throughout the world, and the other franchisers were willing to share information. It was a nice opportunity, and affordable based on what he wanted to spend.

Bob says, "I learned that you have to do due diligence. No broker will tell you all the truth about what you're buying. If you're not cautious and don't take your time, it can be a disaster. I truly lucked out in that courier business process. It was a good lesson. Learn about the business not from the people you're buying it from, but from others in the business, as well as your own common sense. I had never had a small business, but I did have some skills. I'm mechanically oriented, so I could operate the equipment, cash register, etc., but I didn't have skills in managing to the numbers. I just learned by doing, and sometimes by getting burned. For example, in the first three months, month by month, gross sales were getting better and better. I had increased sales over the previous owner's numbers. They were all great growth months. I was euphoric! Then I discovered that I was actually losing money because my labor cost was too high. I wasn't aware of where my costs were and what I had to control. Luckily I had no dream of getting rich quickly, and that's a good thing. People with a financial background would have given it a lot more thought than I did. The costs in some cases surpassed my expectations. One area I didn't consider was air conditioning during the summer. The electricity cost doubled. I also kept the college kids who were already working here over the summer. It was good learning for me — they had the skills and I needed to learn. So, it was a win-win, but more than I had anticipated in cost. I had also hired two individuals anticipating that I was going to open a second store, but that wasn't going to happen at that time. I had to let one of the full timers go. I was much too ambitious about getting started with another store. I needed to get my feet on the ground here first. The time required in the beginning is enormous. 12 hour days. It's better now — only 10 hrs a day and every other Saturday. For the first six to twelve months, it's your life. And it takes awhile to build up to the same amount of income you earned before. But you have other things that can positively impact your tax liabilities…depreciation, etc. So you don't actually have to earn the same amount to come up to your current standard of living".

Bob had been thinking about another store even at the time he bought the first one. He was thinking about the profits — how he might use them for bank loans, etc. Many of the shipping store owners in this area were multiple store owners. Now he's thinking he'll go through the first year, manage funds through the second year, then look for an opportunity to open a new store rather than acquiring an existing one. This was an existing store.

He says, "Things can go wrong — for example a package may be lost. When things like that happen, I put processes in place to prevent them in the future. We only lost two packages over the holidays (doing 200 packages per day). I had a package addressed to an APO, so I ended up sending it through the post office. I forgot to insure it, and ended up losing $1,300 because the package was stolen, lost or whatever. I had another situation where I forgot to insure the package in our system. It was for $30,000. When I realized what I had done, I didn't sleep and I tracked it moment by moment until it reached its destination. It was a near miss. It only takes one of those to sink a business.

It helps to have a great support group. My wife, sister, brother-in-law, and other family members are all supportive. I have joined the Rotary Club, and will probably join the Chamber of Commerce".

Bob's Advice to Others

- When I realized I would need to be making a career change, I went to small business administration courses. My advice is to go to some of these meetings instead of a ball game. Do it even though you may only have a sense that something might happen, and be prepared. Don't go into a hole, don't sit around, get busy. I was spending time every day investigating, talking to people, finding brokers, etc.
- Start by very carefully studying every aspect of the franchise or business you are interested in. One of the best things I did was to interview 8 store owners. Talk to experienced folks and new store

owners. Compare what the new ones are saying with the more experienced ones. Then blend it all together.

- Enthusiasm is important. Don't just be doing it to do it until something else comes along. You need fervor and excitement to make it work. Although this isn't the driving range, my first love, I <u>love</u> this business. Not because I always wanted to have a box company, but because these are great customers! I still serve and solve problems like I did in my former job. That's all part of the fun and the reason for my enthusiasm.

- Other advice is to look at economics, trends, become a futurist if you can. What might change over the next two or three years? Who can you find who can help, who can you talk to? Take the time to do a thorough job of investigating. If someone says something that sounds negative, investigate. Don't close your ears. That worked for me with the courier business.

- Don't underestimate your expenses. If you think things are going to cost x dollars, think again. Is this based on what others are saying, or on your own experience? Keep your eyes and ears open. Little areas make a big difference in the amount of money you're going to make. Not that I was so smart — but I have learned. In my next store, I will apply that experience.

- On funding, if you think you are likely to be laid off, establish as much credit as possible before you lose your job. You can get banks to commit a lot more money if you have an income. If this is going to be a true change of career, get an equity loan or a line of credit. That's usually good for a year or so. It's easier to do this when you're working than when you're not.

Were you able to identify Bob's sense of purpose in his story?

When Bob was consulting, he provided services to his consulting company's clients and enjoyed their high level of satisfaction. When he became a professional development manager, again he was providing services — only to a different set of clients — the consultants. They were very appreciative of Bob's efforts. When he made the decision to go into business for himself, he looked for something in the services industry because he knew he would be able to use his interpersonal skill set and receive the same sense of satisfaction he had enjoyed in his corporate role. His sense of purpose is grounded in providing assistance to others, whether it is his family, his friends or his customers, and through their satisfaction he realizes his own sense of accomplishment.

Food for Thought:

What about your work has been most satisfying to you?

A BLUE WIG AND A TRASH TRUCK

What can make you stop your car in the middle of traffic, smile and nod? A crew of trash collectors wearing blue wigs, standing at an intersection, waving a 6-foot banner at you!

In 2002, Alan Klug was a senior consultant for KPMG, renamed to BearingPoint. He had been with KPMG for five years and loved his work, providing technical consulting services to a variety of clients. Alan derived a high degree of satisfaction from this service business, helping his clients to operate more effectively. He didn't love the travel, however, and that had become the standard operating procedure for his consulting job. In addition, the technical consulting industry was suffering from "economic cardiac arrest", so consulting opportunities were becoming fewer and farther between. The "handwriting was on the wall" indicating that there might not be much opportunity for career growth in consulting in the near future — and definitely not in his own hometown. So Alan thought about what else he might do. A different career? Maybe entrepreneurship? Alan's family owns a uniform (silk screen and embroidery) business, so operating a business was nothing new to him. He knew it would be hard work, but it would also provide some great benefits: more time with his family (he would be at home every night), financial rewards and control over both the direction of the business and his future.

If Alan were going to become an entrepreneur, he wanted it to be a service business. He enjoyed working with his clients. He had considered various possibilities: home services, custom closets, a car wash, quick-serve restaurants, and he had gone so far as to develop business plans for each of them. But none of these really grabbed him. Then he came across a 1/16th page, 250- word sidebar in Fortune magazine for 1-800-GOT-JUNK? Something about it captured his attention. It was so compelling that, in his words, he immediately began researching the heck out of it. There had to be something wrong with this concept — why had no one done this before? If it could be done this way and people wanted the service surely some other nationally branded competition would be in the market. He liked everything 1-800-GOT-JUNK? had to offer, especially their vision and their team approach. So in 2003, with an investment of $60,000, Alan acquired four territories (a territory is a geographic area of about 250,000 people), a truck and four workers, and became a 1-800-GOT-JUNK? franchisee.

For the first year, Alan wore the blue wig and along with his crew headed out at 6:30 am six days a week, driving around, picking up junk, hanging up flyers, returning home at 6:00 pm, spending a couple of hours with his family, then doing paperwork and recruiting of employees from 9:00 p.m. until midnight in his basement office. "It's not easy, but you can do it because you can see your business growing", Alan says. And, as with any business, it also has its entertaining moments, like hauling away the fire hydrant and the bag full of mannequin parts.

Today, he has a staff of twenty, including a full time operations manager and two other managers. His office is outside the house. He goes in at 7:00 am, to get face time with his crews in the morning (he no longer wears the blue wig or picks up trash), and works with his manager to discuss and resolve any HR issues. He handles the accounting, bookkeeping and finance tasks himself. He also manages the relationships with his commercial customers. He is out of the office every day between 9:00 a.m. and 12:00 p.m., working out, taking care of other business and having lunch with his family. He leaves the office by 6:00 p.m. and spends evenings with his wife and two sons, ages two and a half and one. He only works about every third weekend and soon he'll only be working by phone on weekends, so he can enjoy the cartoons with his boys. One of the benefits of his success, is that, if needed, he can take some time during the day to be with them. He also takes at least 1 week of vacation every quarter.

Alan has expanded his territories to eight, and is in negotiation for his ninth. He now has five trucks. He is on track to become a two-million dollar business in 2008, and he is already thinking about what he would like to do next, possibly launch another business.

Alan's advice to others:
- Don't be stuck in a box. All of the same principles you're using as a tech worker can be transferred to other jobs.
- It can be tough moving into a different industry with different interactions. Draw on the processes you know.
- Working for yourself can be a bit strange, because you don't have the same support system you have with a large company. It can be difficult wearing all the hats with no one to fall back on.
- In your own business, you need to be more aggressive, take more risk.
- It's critical to have a plan and stick to it. Talk with others in the same business. Make the effort to be involved with networking groups. Most are more than willing to pass along their experience.
- Understand where you want to go in your life. Alan created his vision

and life purpose when he was in graduate school. Today that guides every decision he makes. He has also worked with coaches to help determine and implement actions to achieve his goals.

- If going into business with partners (buying a franchise is entering into a partnership with the franchisor and its other owners) make sure they are like minded people that you can work and get along with.

- If an opportunity comes along or is found, don't count it out immediately because it is too good to be true, just research it and find all the downsides. There are plenty of opportunities out there just waiting to be exploited.

Reference: Baltimore Business Journal, Cleaning Up a Trashy Industry, Adam Stone, August 22, 2003

How would you describe Alan's sense of purpose?

Alan says his life purpose guides all his decision-making. It focuses on work/life balance, having both time and sufficient financial assets to provide an enjoyable life for his family and himself along with doing work that he perceives as challenging and rewarding, and that adds value to others' lives.

Alan's consulting industry experience was initially a strong reflection of his purpose. When he no longer felt that was possible, he sought out other opportunities.

Food for thought:

What words would you use to describe your relationship to your work? What does your work do for you?

DIFFERENT TASTES

J ack Milan is the eldest of seven brothers, growing up in a middle-class neighborhood in Boston. He was the first in his family to graduate from college. At Northeastern University, he majored in Business Management, and minored in Accounting. He landed a great job right out of college — he was an IT management trainee at Sylvania. He enjoyed IT, and had planned to make it his career, but after awhile he felt that it was taking over his life and he wanted more from life than IT offered. He thought about starting his own business, but he didn't have a clue about what that might be.

While on vacation in California in 1975, he visited Salmagundi, a popular restaurant, where he noticed the difference in restaurant fare from what was customary in Boston at that time. Fitness was a popular trend in California — eating right, exercising, etc. Knowing that trends in America travel from west to east, he saw a potential opportunity. He knew nothing about cooking but he was willing to give it a try, so, with his mother's reluctant assistance (she thought he was crazy), he began to learn how to cook, and he discovered that he actually enjoyed it. He experimented with various recipes at home, practicing in the evenings and on weekends, using his relatives and friends as "focus groups" to provide feedback. Five or six would dine together while completing a survey with questions relating to presentation, first taste, what should be in it, last taste, how does it compare with other similar recipes, etc. From their feedback, Jack refined the recipes, and when he was satisfied they were working, he and his long-time friend, Richard Smenton, launched Stockpot in Boston. It was Boston's first soup and salad restaurant. Success came quickly. Four days into it, it was standing room only! In 1976 they opened a second restaurant in Cambridge and were so successful that others copied their model, the best known of these being Souper Salad. There were offers to write books, to partner in larger ventures, and many to buy the business outright.

While this sounds like the American dream come true, the reality was more negative than positive. It is way more than a 9 to 5 life and it is very hard work. The restaurant business is cyclical, and the owner is the last to get paid. More important, Jack realized that his "synapses were not connecting". He felt that he had a lot of untapped creativity. So he and Richard agreed to sell the business. Richard opened a nightclub in North Easton, while Jack looked for opportunities to further develop his skills and use his creativity.

Through his restaurateur network, Jack met Odette Berry, a well-known Boston caterer. Odette offered Jack an opportunity. He could work with her and expand his horizons through learning the catering business. And he could also learn more about cooking. At that time, Jack, although a successful "chef", had a very limited repertoire. He could only do soups, salads and some baking. In addition to her catering business, Odette also ran a cooking school and Jack participated, taking responsibility for the prep and cleanup. He learned well, and Odette offered him an even greater opportunity — to manage her catering business. She was ready to retire and, when she was confident that Jack was on the road to success, she turned the business over to him. He was only 25 years old and was already on his way to his second successful business.

The business grew and prospered. Jack hired a full-time chef and a sous chef (he can also cook everything himself.) Jack renamed the business Different Tastes, and today it is one of the most prestigious and innovative catering organizations in Boston. Among its clients are Boston's Wang Center for the Performing Arts, the Shubert Theatre and the Massachusetts Institute of Technology (MIT).

> Different Tastes has won many awards. Here are some of them:
> International Catering Company of the Year
> Two Time Winner of National Caterer of the Year
> Sixth Consecutive Catering Company of the Year Award Nomination
> —Event Solutions Magazine
> 2006 Chef of the Year
> 2005 Most Innovative Food Centerpiece
> 2005 Innovative Mixology
> 2004 Most Innovative Food Trend
> 2004 Best Themed Buffet
> 2004 Best Catered Event Under $10,000

Simply stated, Jack loves catering. And he loves sharing his experience with others. He wants people to have the passion he does.

Jack's advice to others:

In a class he taught at Middlesex Community College on "How to Become a Caterer", he said:

"You're continually reinventing and proving yourself. In what other business, when you head out the door, are you one event away from disaster? You're only as good as the last event you've done. Catering is filled with stress. Some people thrive on stress, on overcoming the challenges others fail. If all you have going for you is your love of cooking, don't do it. You most likely won't succeed. And those who do most likely won't get rich, although there are exceptions, i.e., Martha Stewart. But you can be successful. What does it take? You need to be a "realistic optimist". You need to do the analysis, understand the business, understand what you're committing to. You need to believe in yourself, trust your competence, and most important, take control of your life."

How would you describe Jack's purpose?

Jack knew soon after joining the I.T. profession that it wasn't the best fit for him. He felt that his entrepreneurial spirit wouldn't find opportunities for expression in the highly-regimented world of corporate I.T. He combined a spirit of adventure with a love of good food in seeking opportunities to change careers. His purpose in launching his first venture, Stockpot, was to do something no one else had done, through bringing the benefits of the healthier California cuisine to the east coast. In his catering business, Different Tastes, his purpose is to take catering to its highest level by creating great food events that excite both the palate and the eye and provide a foundation for building lasting relationships and memories.

Food for Thought:

What might have happened to Jack if he had decided not to take control of his life, not to try something new but instead had decided to remain in I.T.?

Is there something you've been thinking about trying? What do you think will happen if you never try it?

RAW SILK ROAD

Patricia Adams is on the road to becoming the best jazz singer she can be, pure and simple. But in her past life she took a very different road. She spent thirty-five years in the high-tech industry in human resources, most recently with Digital Equipment Corporation (DEC). When DEC was purchased by Compaq, she says, the "handwriting was on the wall" that many of the corporate functions would be consolidated at Compaq's headquarters. Patricia was eligible for early retirement. She thought, maybe this was the time to take the leap to becoming a serious jazz singer. She had been thinking about this for awhile. She was attending the New England Conservatory of Music and had been considering making music her full-time endeavor.

The decision was actually easy. She sat up in bed one night and realized, "I know what I want to do...I want to sing." She says, "You know, sometimes the universe is so kind to us. So I called my boss and said, "I've decided, if I'm going to make the music work, it's now or never." I had done concerts and recitals, and the DEC family — that's what it was, and still is — was very supportive of me as I was developing my craft. So I left DEC, and then I went through the "Oh, what have I done?" thing. Periodically I would pick up the phone and do something like a musician, but mostly I watched old movies and slept a lot. However, I was able to get past that time because of a lifetime of thinking you must do things seriously, put your head down and do your work."

Patricia says this is because she comes from a family of entrepreneurs. Her parents were in the newspaper and printing business. To understand Patricia's motivation, it helps to understand her parents. Here's their story:

First Alum of Color at Hobart College

(This article, by Kathy Marshall, originally appeared in the Winter 2003 issue of The Pulteney St. Survey and is reprinted her with permission.)

It was September, 1928. A young man arrived in Geneva, having traveled by bus half way across the country from Omaha, Nebraska. The Episcopal Bishop in his home parish had arranged, through an acquaintance with then-Hobart College President Murray Bartlett, for the bright and promising young man to receive a scholarship to attend Hobart College.

Imagine the young man's surprise and dismay when he arrived on campus only to discover that the College would not house him — because he was Black.

Imagine his pride four years later when he graduated, magna cum laude, Phi Beta Kappa, with majors in Greek, English and psychology - the first African-American graduate of Hobart College.

Alger Adams surmounted monumental obstacles to achieve the goals he set for himself.

It was a difficult time for many in this country during the Depression of the early 1930s. Basic survival was challenging for a large portion of the population across the nation. Geneva, N.Y. was no exception. Adams faced not only financial barriers, but also strong racial barriers. He had to find shelter and he had to eat. He turned to the Black community, at that time fewer than 150 in number. Most were domestic help or worked in commercial jobs. Most were poor. But most were eager to help the young man.

Adams' daughter Patricia, a corporate human resources manager turned jazz singer and band leader, remembers some of her Dad's stories of those days.

"When Dad talked about life at Hobart, the talk mostly centered around living in Geneva and trying to make ends meet. He washed dishes at a local restaurant, I know, and lived with various families in the community," she said. "Most of his classmates didn't have to work their way through college, and I remember Dad telling of working on campus, polishing brass fixtures in the hallway of one of the buildings on campus, and being passed by, ignored and unseen by classmates who couldn't touch his excellence when they sat side-by-side in class."

Charles Kenney, a lifelong resident of Geneva, was about 12 when Adams came to town. "I remember Alger quite well, even though he was older and I was, at that time, more interested in basketball than what was going on at the Colleges," Kenney reminisced. "I remember him as a good-looking guy, quiet spoken, and I knew of his problems getting housing."

He became, according to Kenney, a source of genuine pride within the Black community.

For part of his time in Geneva, Adams lived with a family on Dorchester Avenue, within view of Kenney's home. He also spent some time living with Joe and Nettie Dugan on High Street. (The Dugans would later become daughter Patricia's godparents.)

"Everyone was struggling to survive back then, and taking folks into our homes was one way we could make extra money," said Kenney. "Families used to take in the Black performers who came to town, too, because they were not allowed to stay in the local hotels. We had nationally known band leaders, such as Count Basie and others, performing at Club 86, but they had to find alternate housing."

Of the few Hobart or William Smith students who have survived the 70 years since that time, some remember Adams, but they only remember that he was here. "Whites and Blacks didn't mix much in those days," remarked Lib White '33. "Nor was there much mixing between Hobart and William Smith, except for fraternity mixers and occasional dates. In fact, William Smith women were not allowed on the Hobart campus."

And of course Adams didn't live on campus, so even the less formal types of interaction were not common for him.

But he did come to campus for classes and he did excel in the classroom, as his daughter so proudly noted. Not only did he graduate magna cum laude, but he was named to Phi Beta Kappa as well. (Patricia proudly wore her Dad's Phi Beta Kappa ribbon on her lapel during the 2002 Reunion.) He was also an undergraduate assistant in the psychology department and had undergraduate research published in The American Journal of Psychology.

After graduating from Hobart with such distinction, Adams had two clear options: he had been offered a scholarship to the Harvard Graduate School of Business and to the New York Theological Seminary. He chose the latter, based, according to his daughter, not only on his commitment to the priesthood but also on his practical understanding that there was not much an African American could do with an MBA in 1934.

He graduated from the seminary and between 1947 and 1955 he built two churches, St Francis in Greenburgh, N.Y. (now St. Francis & St. Martha's) and St. Augustine's (now, Holy Cross) in Yonkers, N.Y. Both churches recently celebrated their 50th anniversaries and Adams' contributions figured prominently in both celebrations.

In 1950, Adams and his wife, Jessie, purchased a weekly newspaper, the Westchester County Press. Patricia noted that it always bothered him to accept pay for his work in the church, and eventually he left the active ministry. He continued to minister in interim and part-time positions over the years, but at the time he wanted to devote himself to civil rights through the development of the newspaper, which he built to give the African-American community in the county a cohesive voice.

While they were still running the newspaper, the couple developed and built The Creative Printery in 1962. Specializing in the publication of high school and college newspapers in the tri-state area (New York, New Jersey and Connecticut), The Creative Printery offered a teaching environment for students to learn about printing and production. Adams then headed back to academe and earned a master's degree in teaching and studied journalism at which point some colleges accredited the work students performed at The Creative Printery. Adams' ran both the newspaper and the print company through 1980, when he sold The Creative Printery, running the newspaper for three more years before retiring to travel with his wife.

In addition to his many professional accomplishments, Adams wrote two novels, painted 12 oil paintings (10 of which were on display in Houghton House during Reunion 2002), played the piano and the guitar, and was active in a variety of civil rights, professional, and community organizations and initiatives.

No surprise that Hobart College was duly proud of its alumnus. In 1983, Alger Adams was invited to return so that the College could bestow upon him a well-deserved honorary Doctor of Divinity degree.

Patricia noted that her father was thrilled. "He had always been proud to have graduated from Hobart, and for the College to recognize his life's achievements, especially after having in so many real ways rejected him 55 years earlier, was a genuine honor for him," she said.

It was John Witte, long-time Hobart admissions and alumni emissary, who called Adams to the attention of the Board of Trustees. Adams had been a class correspondent since 1979, and Witte had spoken to him at his home, for the first time learning of the circumstances under which Adams had struggled to get his education here, as well as of his later accomplishments, and felt that Adams was a perfect candidate for an honorary degree.

Carroll Brewster, president of the Colleges in 1983, remembers Adams giving a stirring address to those gathered at a dinner in his honor the evening before Commencement in 1983. The citation presented to Adams from Hobart College reads: "...The College, having admitted its first Black matriculate, would subsequently forge a commitment, uncertain at first but later forcefully articulated and resolutely pursued, to encourage and to seek diversity in its student body..."

Adams will now be remembered annually through the Academic Success Dinner. The Office of Intercultural Affairs initiated the dinner last year in order to recognize the achievements of many HWS students who succeed despite financial and academic disadvantage. It is to be held each year "in honor of the first man and the first woman of color to graduate from Hobart and William Smith - The Rev. Dr. Alger L. Adams '32 and Gloria Robinson Lowry '52."

Patricia recently recalled her father's pride in his academic achievements and in his ability to compete successfully with students at Hobart who were more racially, socially and financially advantaged. "I think he was proud of his resourcefulness and skills to survive in an environment where he felt unwanted and discriminated against," she reflected. "But Dad always loved the school and I believe that the school respected him - yet the times interfered. I've come to love the Colleges, too. The welcome was so warm for me at the 2002 Reunion. Everyone went out of their way to greet me and talk to me. It lifted a lot of my sadness about Dad's earlier time here."

In addition to these great accomplishments, Alger Adams was also fascinated by the stock market and was a highly successful investor. Patricia says that his success has made a difference in how she has approached her career. Starting out in a music career, there are very few who initially earn a good living. For Patricia, money has become a tool and a measurement as opposed to something she uses only to live on.

Patricia says she is still developing her style. The thing about the music that's more exciting to her than anything is that her growth is audible to her and everyone else. She has a "personal board of directors" whose members don't hesitate to tell her what they like and what they don't like.

One of her board members is Bill Commerford — he's an artist known for landscapes, who is now becoming known for his water colors of jazz artists. "He's done all the greats — Miles Davis, Stan Goetz. And he did my album covers. In addition to being a portraitist, he's an illustrator, and a marketer. He's really been wonderful in terms of marketing subtleties — like "give away product". I still struggle with that a little bit. My Dad would be horrified.

Bill has helped me understand that sometimes that's a really strategic thing to do."

There have been times when I have said, "I don't know if I can do this". There have been times when I was very, very discouraged. No one in the music business would help me. Vocalists viewed me as competition, and vocalists and instrumentalists are natural enemies. According to one instrumentalist, vocalists get all the gigs. What's probably more realistic is that it doesn't matter how bad or good the vocalist is, it's the vocalist who gets all the attention. I could be on stage with Dave Brubeck, and I'd get the attention. But that's not what I'm about. I'm in the business of making music. I think I would die without the music. It's the only thing I do; it's the only thing I care about. It's the only thing that makes me feel alive and whole. I want people to be able to have a good time. Part of my performance is to walk through the tables between sets and speak to people. Sometimes people want to chat. I learn a lot about who's in the audience. Who's out here and how are they doing? That personal connection is what's important to me."

Here's what the jazz world says about Patricia.

Boston, MA "…A question for all you cynical, sarcastic Jazz fans: What is the last thing you'd expect to run into at a Jazz brunch? Yes. Jazz. But not so fast. I sat down for brunch 2/6 at Ryles and caught Ray Santisi (on acoustic piano!), Marshall Wood and Bob Moses doing what they know how to do superbly. Vocalist Patricia Adams had the good taste to bring along that fine trio and put them to work. It did work. There was plenty of room for them to solo, support and interact. And nobody got in the way of the words. Good thing, too, because Ms. Adams knows about words. The young vocal starlets of the Jazz world today seem to pick up the chestnuts for the first time out of the fake book. But Patricia Adams had these items for breakfast and lunch as a child, living and breathing before some of those tunes saw sunlight. And so when she offers "Ev'ry Time We Say Goodbye", the patina of World War II comes with it. No gimmicks. Just really good music. She's there every first Sunday of the month."

Stu Vandermark, **Cadence Magazine**, April 2005

She has published five albums to date: Raw Silk, Blue For You, Out of This World, With Our Compliments and Live at Ryles Jazz Club, and she is working on her sixth. She is also providing her wealth of knowledge and experience to others at the New England Conservatory of Music.

Patricia's advice to others:
- When you're contemplating a career change, listen to everybody.

Take all the input you can get, but ultimately don't pay attention to anybody but yourself.

- The hardest part is deciding what you want to do. The core issue for many people I worked with as an HR Manager is that they just didn't know. But everything you're doing is tracking to that.

- The real problem for people is that they feel they have lost control. Look inside yourself. Discover who you really are. Discover how you make a difference. Then look for ways to express that difference, to make your own kind of music.

How does Patricia see her life purpose?

Patricia learned who she is through her family. She chose a helping profession, HR, as an expression of her identity. It was a profession in which she could make a difference in the lives of others. And she continues to make a difference to others today through her music, both in her concerts and in sharing her passion with students at the Conservatory.

Food for Thought:

Who are you...really? What will it take for you to find out?

YEAR UP

Gerald Chertavian was born into a typical middle class family in Lowell, MA. His parents provided Gerald and his older brother with a loving, safe and comfortable environment in which to grow up. Life outside his family was somewhat different. A large percentage of the 3500 to 3800 students in the Lowell school system lived below the poverty level. Gerald was acutely aware of the "opportunity divide" between the lifestyle his family enjoyed and that of others who were less fortunate. After graduating from high school, Gerald went on to Bowdoin College. While at Bowdoin, he looked for ways in which he might help the underprivileged. During his freshman summer, he found a job in which he drove "at risk/high risk" teenagers to work duty, raking leaves and cutting grass, often working alongside them, and getting to know them personally. Gerald had always wanted a younger brother, so it was a logical next step for him to become a Big Brother, which he did during his sophomore year.

After graduating from Bowdoin with a degree in Economics, Magna Cum Laude, Phi Beta Kappa, Gerald completed the Harvard Business School MBA program with honors.

He landed a job on Wall Street with the Chemical Banking Corporation, and later as Vice President of Marketing at Transnational Financial Services in London. And he married and started a family.

Throughout this time, he continued to volunteer as a Big Brother. His life experience in New York with his Little Brother made a strong impression. He says, "Not many middle-class people have spent time in a housing project or got to know what it's like to grow up poor in a violent neighborhood." He found himself wanting to do more.

Recognizing that his best opportunity for building a strong financial base for his family and other future activities was entrepreneurship, Gerald co-founded an I.T. communications company, Conduit Communications, in 1993. Conduit grew to $20M in annual revenue and more than 130 employees in London, Amsterdam, New York, and Boston. It was ranked as one of England's fastest growing companies. Although Gerald was considered highly successful, he slowly realized that the business was consuming his life. In 1999, Conduit was sold to i-Cube.

Gerald stepped back to do some soul-searching. He graded himself as a worker and family member and didn't like the grades, so he set about making some changes in his life. He vowed to maintain a healthier work/life balance in the future, and to focus on his passion and purpose: helping disadvantaged young adults. Gerald began desk and field research of various models upon which he could build a program that would make a difference.

He combined his passion and purpose with his entrepreneurial skills, and six figures of his own money to found Year Up in 2000.

Year Up is now in five locations: Boston, Cambridge, Providence, New York City, and Washington, D. C., graduates 500 students per year, and Gerald is raising funds to expand into four more cities. He recently received a commitment of $10 million from Microsoft to assist Year Up's expansion.

Both Fast Company and the Monitor Group have ranked Year Up among the top 25 organizations in the nation using business excellence to engineer social change. Gerald has received a number of awards, including the 2003 Social Entrepreneurship Award by the Manhattan Institute, the 2005 Freedom House Archie R. Williams, Jr. Technology Award and the 2005 and 2007 Social Capitalist Awards by Fast Company and the Monitor Group. He has been featured in many publications, including the Boston Globe, the Boston Herald, BusinessWeek, Fortune Small Business, and Time Magazine as well as The Christian Science Monitor. He serves as a trustee of Cambridge College, Bowdoin College and the Boston Foundation, and is on the Board of Advisors for the Harvard Business School Social Enterprise Club and New Sector Alliance. He was also elected to be an Ashoka Fellow as well as a member of the Young Presidents Organization.

Gerald advice to others:

Take a piece of paper and:

- Write down the ten things you have done that represent success to you.
- Break these down into the individual actions that took place that led to your success — ask yourself what led to your taking these actions.
- Review your actions for patterns.
- Choose to do those things that fit the patterns; those things you have an affinity to or a liking for.
- Find a mentor.

   Gerald says he was fortunate to have Eric Sanquist as a mentor. Eric was a former university professor who taught Gerald to practice "discipline of thought" while he was trying plan his future career path and aspirations.

When asked about "What's next?", Gerald says he will continue to grow Year Up for the next ten years with the ultimate goal of creating a sustainable, scalable organization that has national impact.

Gerald has a strong sense of purpose.

Did you hear Gerald's sense of purpose expressed in his story? It is a driving desire to help those who haven't had the opportunities he was afforded. That desire was evident from the time Gerald was in school, when he began to enact his purpose through the Big Brothers program. And it continues today through his Year Up program.

Food for Thought:

Did you have a driving desire in school? What activities attracted you then? How much time are you devoting to these activities today?

TOMASSO TRATTORIA

Tom Prince was Vice President of Sales for Siebel. When he was given an opportunity to opt out of his role at Siebel with a severance package, he decided to do just that. He had thought from time to time about doing something different with his life, but had never really considered what that might be. He began by taking the summer off. He considered doing nothing, simply retiring early. While he and his wife, Mary, were in a good financial position with Tom's stock from Siebel, he didn't know if he could afford to just not do anything. So Tom thought about becoming a teacher in math or science (he has an engineering degree), and he and Mary also thought about starting a business. The restaurant business seemed like it might be interesting.

Tom says, "We're foodies. We eat out a lot. We love good food. If I was going to be a teacher, I'd have to go back to school, so I dismissed that idea and focused on the restaurant idea. I did a lot of reading and I met a guy named Lorenzo Savona. He has tons of experience in the restaurant business and was looking to open the same kind of restaurant we were thinking about. Honestly, without him, we couldn't have launched Tomasso Trattoria. I didn't come into this with any prior experience. I did a lot of due diligence and developed a business plan. Mary and I have lived around here for twenty years. We knew the local market well, so we didn't need to do a lot of market research. I wanted to have a business that didn't require me to be here all the time. A smaller business would have been less risky, but a smaller business would also have required a lot more of my time. We're always at risk here for that to happen, if a key person were to leave, but Mary and I can fill in if there are gaps in the schedule. We both work at the restaurant and our store, Panzano Provviste e Vino, every day so we are able to wear many hats and step in whenever needed, which includes everything from taking reservations, expediting and servicing food and managing the front of the house during service."

Tom and Mary are versatile, but they can't fill in for their kitchen staff. Tom says, "I know how to cook, but there's not a lot of relationship between what you do in cooking at home and cooking in a restaurant kitchen. It's a very fast pace. The kitchen staff are all young and they're also well trained. We can't hire someone to do this job who comes in and says I want to learn how to be a cook. It's so demanding that we need experienced people". Tom had really never thought about being the chef. He does, however, enjoy being involved in planning the menu, with everything made from the best ingredients.

Mary says, "One of the reasons Tom wanted to do this was to give our daughters the opportunity to work in a family business. One of our daughter's college essays was about the experience of working in the business. The girls like having their dad around and he has a lot of flexibility that he didn't have when he was on the road selling software. He can help them with homework, he can take them to school in the morning, and to other activities. And they've really gained an appreciation for food. We took them to Italy five years ago and again last fall. Visiting Italy made us realize what we were missing back home when it came to food. It started there". Indicating the pictures on the wall, she says, "These photographs are from our trip to Tuscany. What's important about Tomasso Trattoria, and our new market and wine shop, Panzano Provviste e Vino, is the care and love behind everything we serve and sell, ranging from our house-made breads and organic meats raised on family farms, for example, to our wines, many produced in small quantities, many organic, and all the finest vintages".

Tom says. "There's so much disillusionment in high-tech. You rarely get the feeling that you're selling people something they really want. And I was dealing with the other side of the coin, people who bought too much and wanted to give it back. I was dealing with purchasing people and executives who were never going to use the product themselves. It was fun doing the deals, but the product was then handed off to the people who actually used it. The people I dealt with didn't have that much interest in it. Here, we're providing something that people actually know and care about - something that people really want. Food affects their sight, their smell, their taste, their touch, all of their senses."

One of the surprises Tom and Mary had was the staffing issue. The people that are involved in the restaurant industry are a lot different from those in hi-tech. They have a different mindset, a different way of viewing things. Here, some people are looking at this as a temporary job. Some are in school. Even the highest paid here don't make as much as an entry level person in hi-tech. People who make close to that money here are highly skilled — they're at the top in what they do. In this industry, people can easily go out and find another comparable job. People in hi-tech are in some sense overpaid for what they do, and that's probably why they don't leave".

He continues, "For the entrepreneur, in other kinds of restaurants — franchises — you can make more money. But you sacrifice a lot of what we value here: great food made from scratch with only the finest ingredients, high quality service, and a beautifully unique atmosphere. We had to switch gears for the restaurant business. Moving from hi-tech to the restaurant business is like moving from virtual to sensual. Hi-tech was virtual. The restaurant is hands-on, sensual, constantly in reactive mode where stuff is happening in real time all the time".

Tom discovered that they couldn't use the same management processes as in hi-tech. He says, "I wasn't used to getting bombarded, getting interrupted all the time. At Siebel, it was much more deliberate. Here it's sort of frantic — high energy. The customer is here. You have to make a decision while they're here. Everything happens at a faster pace. Every minute, things are happening that you have to react to. You can't think about how to do it perfectly. You just get it as close to perfect as you can".

Mary is responsible for marketing (she was formerly a Marketing Communications executive in hi-tech). Tom handles the finances, controlling the business from a financial perspective. He's involved in all of the operational decisions. He says, "Sometimes I grab plates and run them out to seats, and at other times I deal with issues someone is having. I'm usually in by 10:00 a.m. and leave by 6:00 p.m. Mary works in both the store and the restaurant managing things, taking care of guests and customers, and meeting with the chefs and managers regularly to direct our marketing efforts. The actual hours don't seem like much, compared to high tech careers, but they're intense hours. At Siebel, I might be there for 10 or 12 hours, and it could be draining sometimes, but you could pace yourself. Here it's very draining. Most shifts are five or six hours at a time, and for most, that's all they can do. Some of our chefs and servers work double shifts. It's hard. You're in front of customers all the time. You step out on the floor and you immediately feel the pressure to make sure that everything is going right and on time. If you forget one table, those people are very upset. You have to make it the right way and serve it the right way every single time. And we're open seven days a week. In the summer, we're closed on Sundays, and I reduce my schedule to come in only two or three times a week. During the week, we serve lunch and dinner. The store is open every day. I have this program that allows me to log in from home — that helps in the summer. There are things that I do need to be here for — going to the bank, paying the bills, etc.

Tom continues, "I'm looking forward to growing the business. We recently opened our new Tuscan market & wine shop, Panzano Provviste e Vino, next door. I'm looking forward to seeing the store doing really well. We have thought about opening another restaurant, but Tomasso is not something that can be replicated. People don't understand how unique it is. You can't standardize this kind of a place. It's just not possible. We like the Mario Batali model where each restaurant is different, with different price points, different menus, different kinds and levels of service. That's a possibility for us in the future, to have several restaurants with a common theme, but differentiation. And it will always be us and Lorenzo. We couldn't do it without him".

Tom's and Mary's advice to others:
- Mary says, "You only live once. Life is short. You need to find purpose, love in your life. If a dish here doesn't survive out on the floor, it's because it wasn't made with love. You need to think about what you really like, what interests you, what you bring to the table, what you can leverage.
- Most unsuccessful entrepreneurs have poor business management and a lack of capital. We weren't chefs, we didn't know a lot about wine, we didn't know a lot about the restaurant business, but at least we had management skills and capital. Capital is a big hurdle for many. And when we're young, a lot of us are so scared. We go to college, and we know we have to make money when we get out. I.T. attracts us for that reason. But there needs to be something more. I tell my daughter, who's applying for college now, to do something she really enjoys and that, combined with tenacity, will lead to success naturally.
- Tom says, "Before I left Siebel, I thought it would be nice not to do what I was doing, but I couldn't think of anything I wanted to do. I didn't have the time or inclination to think about it while I was working. Mary adds, "For me, this was a continuation of what I wanted to do. I had the good fortune to take some time while in college to identify writing and marketing as my passion. And it helps to be an eternal optimist. Tom is an eternal optimist. But we did a lot of planning, too. We identified and quantified the risks. And it all worked out!"

How would you express Tom and Mary's purpose?

For Tom and Mary, their purpose is fueled by passion for their family and their love of good food, which they expressed in moving away from the virtual and reconnecting with the sensual, truly living life, working together and enjoying the challenges and rewards of entrepreneurship through Tomasso Trattoria and Panzano Provviste e Vino.

Food for Thought

Are you living only in a virtual world? Are you standing by, or are you living life to its fullest? What would it take to do so?

LEAF AND PETAL

J *oyce Gubata's dream of a floral and gift shop offers an enjoyable, sensory-oriented experience. While many floral shops have some gift items, very few offer enough to create a leisurely shopping experience. Leaf & Petal's unique environment for the senses does just that, offering unique gift items, silk stems and arrangements, fresh flowers, potpourri, gourmet chocolates, off-beat greeting cards and much more, all in a warm, welcoming environment.*

Leaf & Petal blends the beauty and fragrance of nature in the flower shop with an assortment of unique gifts. Leaf & Petal provides patrons with a quiet escape from the world, creating a place where shoppers can stop and smell the flowers, literally and figuratively.

Leaf & Petal's shopping experience goes beyond a bouquet of flowers. Store shelves are stocked with unusual and hard-to-find items that reflect the uniqueness of the shop. High-end edible treats and goodies, gourmet coffees and teas, original artwork and home décor from local artisans showcase the personality of Joyce, and through her, Leaf & Petal.

For those not blessed with a green thumb, gorgeous silk flowers and arrangements supplement Leaf & Petal's exquisite fresh varieties. Floral consultations on either fresh or silk flowers explain the significance and meaning of different blooms, as well as how to create your own arrangements for large-scale events or home decoration".
- from www.leafpetal.com

Seems like a long way from I.T., doesn't it?

Joyce Gubata had a great career in I.T, but it wasn't her first choice. When she graduated from high school, she went into nursing school. After a year and half, she realized that nursing wasn't for her. Her father had served in the U.S. Air Force, and told great stories about his experiences. She decided that she would try the Air Force and after much aptitude testing they told her that she was to "stay away from anything mechanical", and instead attend Czech language school in Monterey, CA. After completing language school, she was assigned to Germany for over 2 years, then outside Washington, D.C. for the remainder of her total of 7 years with the Air Force. During her enlistment, she took computer science and business classes through the University of Maryland.

Joyce left the Air Force in 1984, at about the time the tech industry boom was taking off, and earned a certificate in Data Processing through Computer Data Institute. She married John and settled in the Washington, D.C. area. She was hired by JAYCOR not for her data processing skills, but for her security clearance. She served in several different roles in the D.C. area.

When Joyce and her husband relocated to the Boston area, she went to work for Children's Hospital, in Clinical Applications. As with many organizations, there were political conflicts at the hospital. When her manager left, his staff was also impacted. Joyce was laid off. She was taken by surprise, and realized that this was a serious situation, so she made "looking for a job" her job. She worked closely with a great recruiter, and was hired by Arbella Insurance in December. She was delighted and to celebrate, Joyce and her family: John, Eric and Laura, went to Disney World the week before Christmas.

After three years, Joyce grew restless and left Arbella. She decided that consulting would be a great opportunity in which to use her skills and also to acquire new ones, along with variety in assignments. She was hired by Arthur Andersen Business Consulting. She was there for a year, and then joined a small consulting start-up, Aperio. She was employee #17. After six months, Aperio was acquired by BroadBase Software, with Aperio acting as their East Coast service provider. BroadBase acquired a CRM company, ServiceSoft, and moved its east coast staff into ServiceSoft's headquarters. Then, BroadBase merged with Kana Software, taking the Kana name.

There were now 1500 employees in the organization and Joyce became Director of Consulting for the East Coast. Unfortunately this was the beginning of the tech downturn. One of Joyce's first responsibilities was to lay off a number of staff. She says, "It was one of the hardest things I have ever done". As a result of the merger, 25% of the staff were let go, either to eliminate duplication of effort, or because of the downturn. What helped Joyce get through this was knowing that those who were laid off received good severance packages, not always the case in the industry.

The BroadBase culture was very different from Aperio. Aperio was a collaborative, caring culture. BroadBase was a highly competitive, almost war-like culture. It was all about conquest, winning the golden idol. Joyce says, "The BroadBase culture persisted through the Kana merger. It wasn't what I had signed on for at Aperio. It was not a fun place to be, but I was being well paid, and the market wasn't good, so I stayed on".

Kana decided to outsource their consulting work to their strategic partners, Andersen Consulting, BearingPoint, and IBM, among others. Joyce realized that her job was going to change significantly, so she lobbied for and won a new opportunity: partner enablement. She then moved into the Sales/ Engineering group. Unfortunately, their leader was ineffective, and the group struggled. Joyce didn't see any opportunity for career growth. She was working mega-hours and hating it. She thought, "This is what the Corporate world is like, but what else can I do?"

While working full-time, Joyce had also earned an MBA from Northeastern University. She thought about the possibility of going into business for herself. She investigated further and after considerable market research, she decided on a business that focused on flowers and gardens because she enjoyed gardening herself.

Leaf and Petal opened on November 1, 2004. At first, a part of the business focused on container gardens. Her idea was to have a place where home gardeners could create their own container gardens without having to move the heavy bags of potting soil and fertilizer. Unfortunately, the people who composed her target market went to the Cape for the summer, so she abandoned that idea. Then she decided to add gifts to the florist side of the business. This went very well.

Joyce also included a small café, with coffee, muffins, breads and light lunches, and she talked her husband into running it. They opened the café on December 1st. The date happened to coincide with Midnight Madness, an annual Christmas event in Medfield in which the Main Street stores stay open until midnight. Joyce and her husband decided to sell hot chocolate for 50 cents a cup — the best hot chocolate in the area, by the way. Joyce was participating in a fair in another town that evening, so her husband and a newly hired high school student were "on their own". Initially, they didn't have many customers. They moved their sign to the top of the street to attract more business and it worked. They were inundated! Joyce returned from the fair at around 10:30 pm to learn that the shop had a line of customers out the door and up the street. It was a great beginning. Unfortunately, Joyce discovered that it was a lot tougher to run multiple businesses than she had thought. She began looking for someone to take over the café and is now in the final stages of completing their arrangement.

After 2 years, Joyce realized that, while the business was growing rapidly, one shop would not have enough sales volume to achieve her five-year business goals, so she began looking for a second, more visible location. She seriously considered the former Gallo location in Walpole, but that fell through. Instead, she settled on the old blacksmith shop. It's a great location with approximately 25,000 cars per day passing by. The only glitch was that they wouldn't allow food, but the market was such a good one for a gift shop, that Joyce decided to go ahead with just gift and floral. The Walpole Leaf and Petal opened in June 2007, and Joyce is confident that it will help her achieve her five year goals.

"I'm passionate about retail", she says. "People told me I was crazy to be considering retail — that I'd be working all the time. That didn't frighten me, because I was already working mega-hours. I'm used to doing hard work. But this isn't really like work to me — it's way too much fun to be called work. Statistics say that 50% of new businesses fail…I've thought about what I would do if I didn't make it. Initially I thought I could always go back to a corporate role, but now I won't say that. I'm confident that Leaf and Petal will make it, but if the unexpected happens, I'll find another business. I'm really an entrepreneur at heart! "

Joyce's Advice to Others:

- I have been able to leverage much of what I learned in the corporate world, especially my project management skills.

- I have more of a head for business vision and strategy than I do for the mechanics of the business. As an entrepreneur, I have to do everything, or hire people to do it for me. So I hire good people to do Those things that I'm not good at.

- I discovered that I don't have to be perfect. You have to allow yourself to make mistakes and, in fact, expect that you will make many. Too many entrepreneurs beat themselves up over mistakes. Instead, just learn from your mistakes and go on. It's critical to your well-being to let it go, no matter what the impact of the mistake and how much you wish you hadn't made a particular decision or had handled a situation differently.

- I'm able to zig and zag — to recognize and take advantage of opportunities when they come. You have to be ready to bend and sway, to shape-shift, to change. There is one rule that you MUST live by — you have to do what your customers want, not what you want. Stay tuned to what they like about you and what they don't, and do a survey at least once per year asking what they want.

- Most of all, it's important to be passionate about what you do. I'm passionate about working with "real, down-to-earth" people. We go to floral design shows, and the designers all hug each other — they're involved emotionally. I felt like I had lost who I was in the corporate world. I'm now able to be myself — a woman. In the corporate world of the '80's, women modeled their dress and behavior after men because they were trying to succeed in a man's world. We felt the need to blend in, hide our femininity, and even believed that to be feminine was to be weak and frivolous. Today, it's very different. Women aren't afraid of the workplace anymore, or of being women, and in fact are setting their own rules. I find now that I absolutely rejoice in being a woman and love associating with other women. I've recently joined NEWBO (the New England Women Business Owners), where I will participate in CEO Roundtables. It's empowering, liberating. Women in business have finally come into their own.

This poem, that Joyce has adopted as "the company poem", beautifully expresses the essence of Leaf and Petal, and of Joyce Gubata.

If of they mortal goods thou art bereft
And from thy slender store
Two loaves alone to thee are left
Sell one, and with the dole,
Buy hyacinths to feed the soul.

From the Gulistan of Moslih Eddin Saadi
13th Century Persian Poet

What is Joyce's purpose in life?

Joyce found her true self in entrepreneurship. In the corporate world, she was stifled. She was successful, but she wasn't satisfied with her success. Success came at a significant price — the suppression of her true self — a price she was no longer willing to pay. Her purpose is to express her true self, enabling others to do the same.

Food for Thought:

What about you? In your current role, are you able to be who you truly are, or do you find yourself playing a role each day that isn't really you? What would need to happen for you to more effectively express your true self?

TOOLIE THE TRAVEL GUIDE™

Jocelyn Garner didn't set out to pursue a career in I.T. She was a music major in college, where she became friends with a computer science professor who gave her a spur-of-the-moment opportunity to try out the profession. A program had been deleted from the system, and he offered Jocelyn the task of re-entering it. The program was many pages of code, and would require a considerable effort to re-enter, but Jocelyn was game. The professor gave her his access code, and escorted her down to the inner-sanctum, the computer room. Hours later, she was still keying in code when several programmers spotted her, asked her who she was and what she was doing there and peremptorily escorted her upstairs. She explained that she was helping the professor, and expressed an interest in working with computers. Jocelyn was offered and accepted a job as an operator. She had unexpectedly landed one of the best paying jobs on campus and held it for two years, until she graduated with a degree in music education.

After graduation, she first taught in a private school, then went on to graduate school in music. Her day jobs in IT helped pay for expensive voice lessons. A friend recommended her as a potential technical writer, and she accepted a job with Ashton-Tate (the creator of dBase). Subsequent work as a technical writer led to a job with Microsoft in 1993. As a technical writer, she participated in the development of the C++ documentation. She was later offered the opportunity of joining the C++ development team as a samples developer, and was the first female developer on that team. The programmer who trained her had to do so after-hours to escape the snide remarks of the others who felt that a previously untrained developer didn't belong. Despite the prevalent attitude, Jocelyn was successful. She later moved from a development role to testing, and then to project management. She also enjoyed the role of conference speaker for Visual C++ and the Windows team, while traveling extensively for the company.

She knew that she had advanced as far as she could at Microsoft without moving into management, and she knew that management wasn't what she wanted, so she began to think about what else she might do with her life.

Jocelyn took two years to work out her new career direction. She loved to travel, to speak and to write. She thought about how she might combine these talents and skills to create a business. Jocelyn decided to publish travel guides, but not those that are commonly used by leisure travelers today. Her travel guides would specifically target the business traveler. She had "been there, done that", and understood the frustrations that business travelers experience in trying to make their way in unfamiliar surroundings, under serious time pressure. Her guides would be written from her experience, not sitting at a desk, but actually traveling, experiencing the issues and problems that all business travelers face. Her guides would be user-friendly and downloadable so that business travelers could always have the latest information at their fingertips.

And she would create her own publishing company, marketing her guides to organizations and convention centers, and become a featured speaker on the experience of traveling for business.

These two years were truly an empowering process for Jocelyn. She made detailed lists of all the things that Microsoft provided for her as a business person, then made plans on how she'd either replace them or do without them.

After leaving Microsoft, Jocelyn developed a plan for building her business by working with a branding specialist, where the names Tooliedotter Press™ and Toolie the Travel Guide™, were born (and later trademarked). Toolie was her grandmother's nickname. Her grandmother was the matriarch of the family, a role model to all its female members. Jocelyn was a bit reluctant to assume her grandmother's nickname (it would be difficult to live up to, she thought), but her family encouraged and supported her in doing so. Jocelyn's first publication was her father's book, "Beyond Church — The Gospel in American Life" (by E. Lincoln Pearson), http://www.beyondchurch.com.

Unfortunately, Jocelyn's mother was dying of Alzheimer's as she began to implement her plan, so progress on her plan was somewhat slower than she had intended. She was fortunate to have an Internet Marketing mentor who helped her learn how to operate on the Internet. She also drew on a virtual peer group for information and support. The result is that she is well on her way. She has deployed her website (http://www.tooliethetravelguide.com), and is working on the first ten guides that will be released next year. She also joined the local chapter of the National Speaker's Association, NSA Northwest, and later became its President.

She hasn't regretted leaving I.T. In a sense, she feels like she never left. She's the network administrator for her home network of six PCS and three Macs. And she created her NSA Chapter's website, http://www.nsanorthwest.org. She says, "It's always hard to keep up with the latest technology, but keeping up for the sake of keeping up is less important to me now. My focus isn't so much on the technology itself, it's on how the technology can support my business. I teach business travelers to apply technology so they can be productive."

Jocelyn's advice to others:

- "If you decide to start your own business, focus on that first before you do any volunteer work or add activities to your life. The transition from employee to entrepreneur is a significant mindset shift, and you need to concentrate on making that work first. Once you have your business working, there will be plenty of time to give to others outside your business and family circles.

- Get a mentor in your field whom you can respect, and let them help you from the beginning. Following someone else's model for success is the quickest way to your own. You can customize and enhance their model to fit your own style as you go.

- Get plenty of sleep! Make time to relax, and enjoy that time. There's no point in leaving a stressful job to start your own business and then becoming stressed out about that! Above all, make your passion your business — then it truly feels like play."

Did you spot Jocelyn's purpose?

It may not have been immediately apparent, but Jocelyn's decision to leverage her skills helped her to identify and enact her purpose. She could have easily been entrapped by the barriers life presented her, but she chose instead to focus outward. Through reaching out to others and leveraging the skills she had acquired through her business travel experience, she crafted her business model and found satisfaction and joy through service to others.

Food for Thought:

What's getting in your way? What barriers are preventing you from identifying and enacting your life purpose? What can you do to eliminate them?

LOVE AT FIRST BITE

Marissa Rosenfield Smajlaj is both a technical professional and an artist. During college, she studied costume design, illustration, animation and graphic design. She graduated from Pennsylvania State University in 1993 with a degree in Integrative Arts. After Penn State she began working as a receptionist for Catalink Direct, an electronic computer products catalog, later moving into the role of Catalog Production Assistant in which she was responsible for maintaining the catalog. Unfortunately there wasn't much opportunity for artistic self-expression.

During that time, she also held a part-time job as a waitress and discovered that she really enjoyed working with people and food. She decided to "quit her day job to focus on the restaurant thing" along with some opportunities as a freelance muralist. But in 1997 she realized that while she truly enjoyed what she was doing, it wasn't "paying the bills", so she took a job at Elcom Systems as a Catalog Production Assistant, where she was responsible for designing and maintaining their catalogs and their internal and external website. She also trained their clients in Europe. Marissa decided she needed to broaden her graphics experience, so she began looking for other opportunities. In 1999 she began working for Keane, Inc., as a graphic designer.

Then, in late 2000, she had an epiphany — she "discovered pastry". She was shopping in a bookstore in downtown Boston, and came upon Colette's Birthday Cakes, by Colette Peters. Colette Peters is a world-renowned specialty cake artist and author. As Marissa turned the pages, admiring each design, she thought, "I could do this!" Over the next few days, she couldn't stop thinking about the book and wondering what she might do to test her assumption. She found an opportunity to work part time at a bakery and for a dessert caterer. She couldn't afford to leave her graphic design role, so she made an arrangement with her manager, whereby she could work at the bakery in the early morning (beginning at 6:00 am) several mornings a week and on Saturdays before going to work at her "real job." It was love at first bite!

Marissa began researching culinary schools and focused on the "best of the best", Le Cordon Bleu in London. She had lived in London for a time during college and still had friends there. Family and friends suggested that she also consider other schools, but she felt strongly that Le Cordon Bleu was where she needed to be. She applied and was accepted, but then realized that she needed to bankroll more money before making the move, so she went to live with her parents in Florida — the week before September 11th, 2001. She says deciding to defer her acceptance to culinary school was the best decision she could have made, given the circumstances.

She began the Le Cordon Bleu Diplôme de Patisserie program in May of 2002, completing it in March of 2003. While in the program, she worked at a London restaurant and became good friends with one of the chefs, Aleksander Smajlaj. Their friendship developed into a romance. In June 2003 they married in his home country, Albania, and struggled through the mountains of paperwork needed for him to come to the U.S. Marissa returned to Florida without Aleks and began working as a waitress and a pastry chef in a local restaurant. It was a great learning experience, giving her the practice she needed to build her skills. She says, "At the beginning, only about 50% of what I made was up to my standards and actually saleable, but over time I improved so much that it was difficult to keep up with the demand, and the restaurant raised their dessert prices." During the restaurant's yearly closing of the month of September, she took the opportunity to spend that time with a friend from culinary school in California, helping her migrate her cheese business to pastry. From that experience, Marissa learned that she wanted to have her own business at some time in the future.

Aleks came to the U.S. in December 2003. Initially they worked together in Florida, then in June 2004 they moved to New York City where he had family and friends. Aleks found a job right away, and Marissa found one two months later. She became Assistant Pastry Chef at The Riverdale Garden, which gave her the opportunity to continue doing what she loved and to work on perfecting her skills. In November, she became a Chocolatier with SweetBliss by Ilene C. Shane — producing a huge line of gourmet chocolates. By venturing into a different area of the dessert world, she developed a newfound love and passion for working with chocolate and gained a wealth of experience.

But her greatest production, along with Aleks, was in July, 2005, when their son, Jeston, was born. The family moved to Boston in December, 2005, when Aleks was transferred from his job in NYC to the Boston restaurant of the Smith and Wollensky Restaurant Group and also began working as a cook in a Boston hotel. Marissa did some freelance birthday cakes and pastry work while caring for Jesse.

In late 2006, she was ready to go back to full-time work and began looking for her next opportunity. Online and in a local newspaper, she read the biography of a woman who had started her own Personal Chef business and she thought, "I'd really like to meet her". Then in February 2007, while Marissa and Aleks were car shopping, they visited a Honda dealership. As fate would have it, Marissa immediately recognized the woman sitting in the cubicle next to theirs, also car shopping. It was the same woman whose bio she had read just a couple of days earlier. She introduced herself and the result is that they are planning to work together.

Marissa's Advice to Others:

- Marissa says she knew early on that graphic design wasn't for her. It was safe — it paid the bills. While watching a friend go through a serious illness, seeing his struggle, she realized that "life is too short to only "play it safe"". She believes this was her defining moment.

- She says: Find your passion and pursue it. Research what you're drawn to. Read books, magazines, search online — get as much information as you can. Even if it's not the right time financially or you're afraid to take that leap at that moment, keep working at fine-tuning your skills and learning as much as possible about your chosen industry. Eventually, the time will be right, and you'll be ready. And, it's never too late!!

- Find professionals in the field you're interested in, become a sponge, ask questions — no question is too small. "I was fortunate to have great teachers at Le Cordon Bleu. One of them was a Pastry Chef at Harrods Department Store in London.

- Find opportunities to try out your chosen role. There's nothing like reality to test your dream. Starting to work at 6:00 a.m. with five projects going all at once — that was a true test, and I just knew it was right for me!"

Marissa found her passion and sense of purpose — did you catch how it happened?

Things often happen when you least expect them. Marissa found her passion while browsing in a bookstore. She paid attention to what resonated within her as she was perusing Colette Peters' book. She took the risk to try out what she was drawn to and learned from that experience that it was the right direction for her. Her passion became her purpose through Le Cordon Bleu and was later reflected in both her personal and professional life — her marriage, the birth of her first child and her opportunities to grow as a pastry chef.

Food for Thought:

Is there something you've been thinking of trying out, but you just haven't been able to take the risk? What's preventing you? Is there a way to do it without "giving up your day job"? Remember — "Of all sad words of tongue or pen, the saddest are these: It might have been."

TEE TIME

In the 70's, Bill Sobbing graduated from college in Chicago with a B.A .in English. Like so many other college grads, he hadn't decided what he wanted to do with his life, so landing a job was difficult. He applied for a number of opportunities without success. A relative in Omaha who had connections with the Union Pacific railroad helped Bill get a job in the rail yard, building rail cars. From there, he moved inside to the mailroom. The I.T. Department posted an entry-level programming job opportunity. The money was good, so Bill decided to apply. He passed the screening test and was hired. His I.T. career began with a 3-week training course in which he learned COBOL along with other technical skills.

Bill had worked as programmer for three + years when he decided that he wanted to relocate away from the "snow belt". He chose Arizona, saved up money, sold his house and moved. He enrolled in the Arizona State University MBA program, graduating in 1985. Bill began working for ITT Courier, supporting their accounting systems. Then ITT Courier was bought out by IDEA. With the resulting culture and management changes, Bill decided he no longer wanted to work there. He accepted a programming position with Best Western and worked his way up to manager. Best Western went through a restructuring process, once again with significant changes that Bill disliked, so he looked for a new opportunity.

He was hired by ViaSoft as a consultant. He was excited about the opportunities for greater variety and to work directly with clients. His previous positions had all been "back office". In 2000, ViaSoft was acquired by Allen Systems Group (ASG) and in 2001, Bill, along with many others, was laid off.

Bill had recently attained a PMP certification through the Project Management Institute, so he decided to leverage these skills and go into business for himself as an independent consultant. One of his clients was his former employer, Best Western. They offered him a permanent position, but he turned them down. He decided to move away from the big-business environment, and instead began marketing his consulting services to small businesses. In addition, he began teaching management and systems development courses at the University of Phoenix.

Teaching and consulting to small businesses was rewarding, but the marketing aspect of consulting was problematic. It was difficult to balance sales and delivery, so he decided to return to the world of big business consulting. Bill joined Ajilon, consulting with Wells Fargo Bank in San Francisco. In 2002, he traveled back and forth between San Francisco and Phoenix, and he was able to work remotely from home on occasion. In 2003, he primarily worked from home. While working from home was convenient in many ways, he missed the sociability of working with others, and he realized he wasn't finding much satisfaction in simply doing the "same old, same old". While on vacation, he stepped back and thought about this dissatisfaction and decided that after vacation he would make some changes.

One morning, he picked up the newspaper and read a story about a local school, San Diego Golf Academy, that offered a golf course management training program. He had played golf casually since he was in high school and enjoyed the game, but he had never considered making it a career. There was something about the story that captured his attention, however, so he decided to check it out further. He enrolled as a Golf Academy student in January, 2004 and completed the program in April, 2005. He says,"I learned not only how to manage a golf course, but I also improved my golf swing!"

Since then, he has worked for several AM Golf Corporation courses in the Phoenix area. He started at the bottom — his first job was with a small course, on the closing shift. In his next job, he successfully managed golf tournaments at larger courses. Today, he is Assistant General Manager of one of Scottsdale's oldest courses. His goal is to have his own 9-hole course one day.

He says," I was tired of chasing the technology, trying to keep up with the latest developments. There were always guys out there who marketed themselves as experts, who were ready to move in to your job. Sure, the money was better in I.T., but in what I.T. jobs can you enjoy the blue sky and the sunshine, drive around on the grass, and play a few holes of golf?"

Bill's advice to others:
- Training, whether in your current I.T. job or focused on a new direction, is always valuable, and not just for the learning. Community colleges are great places to build relationships. The people you meet can provide assistance and opportunities. They can become an extended support group, in addition to your family and friends.
- It's easy to leave I.T. when you're laid off. It can be hard to voluntarily leave I. T. if you've become accustomed to the money. If you're not enjoying your job, find something you do enjoy. Figure out what you really want to do, and do it — don't just follow the money.

What about Bill's sense of purpose?

Does Bill just want to spend time on the golf course, or is there also a sense of passion and purpose in his story? Bill loves golf. And he loves it not only for its own sake, but also for the relationships he builds while playing. There are opportunities for relationship-building within I.T., but they're not the same as those built under an expanse of blue sky, on a carpet of green, in the spirit of friendly competition. Bill not only loves golf, he also loves providing that soul-refreshing experience to others.

Food for Thought:

Is there something you love that you also love providing to others? Is there some way that might become a foundation for a different career direction?

LETTERS BY LINDA

Linda Reardon grew up in Pennsylvania. She met her future husband in college, and was a second semester junior when they married. Her husband joined the Army, and they had their first baby. He was discharged from the Army in 1971 and their second baby came along in 1973. Linda subsequently went back to college. She had originally majored in Library Science, but was no longer as interested in that field, so she changed her major to Business. A core requirement for her Business major was Introduction to Computer Science, and...she fell in love!

Upon graduating in 1981, she went to work for Quaker State in their I.T. department. She was with Quaker State for eight years. Next, she joined an I.T. consulting firm, Computer People, serving Blue Cross of Western Pennsylvania. The family moved to Alabama because her husband, a banker, had been laid off, and he was offered a job at SouthTrust Bank. Linda also obtained a job there with no prior banking experience. They offered her the job because they had a project "with the clock running" and she had the experience they needed for the project. She was successful, and they subsequently made her a project manager. She thoroughly enjoyed working for SouthTrust. It was like an extended family. Everyone had family pictures on display and knew about each other's children and grandchildren. It was very difficult for everyone when SouthTrust merged with Wachovia and so many people were let go. Linda stayed until the "bitter end" because SouthTrust provided a great severance package. She received six months of outplacement support and a significant bonus.

During the months preceding her release, Linda thought about what she might do with the rest of her life. At age 53, Linda had started Tae Kwon Do karate to boost her self-confidence. She had become a third-degree black belt. She had competed in national competitions, ranking in the top ten in her division. And she had noticed the embroidery on her karate school's uniforms. She was drawn to the embroidery because, when she was growing up, her grandmother had taught her sewing. She had continued sewing throughout her life as a hobby, including making some of her own children's clothing. She decided that she could leverage her sewing skills to start a home-based business. And so Letters by Linda was born! She purchased a $20,000 computer-driven embroidery machine to do custom embroidery of uniforms, hats, shirts, and other items.

She is successful in part because she can provide faster turnaround than the larger embroidery firms — typically less than two weeks. With the larger firms, small orders are pushed to the back of the production schedule.

This business is ideal for Linda because it allows her to schedule her own time. She enjoys spending time with her grandchildren, even driving a carpool for one of them. And Linda's husband is her biggest cheerleader - he's behind her 100%! He even went to school with her to learn how to use the embroidery machine, to be available to her as a back-up. Although Linda has stopped competing in karate, she's still attending classes. And she does the embroidery for the school's karate uniforms.

Linda's advice to others:
- Explore; consider what's possible.
- Find and do what you love. Discover what makes you happy, satisfied, content, even if others may consider it to be "off the wall."
- Be prepared for the effort required. Having your own business, especially in start-up, may require more time and effort than you think.
- Customer satisfaction is critical to your success. Your customers are your best source of advertising. I recommend joining Business Network International, a group of small business owners that help each other through providing information, support and business leads.
- Keep your options open. Recently I earned a PMP certification from the Project Management Institute. I'm anticipating turning a profit this year, but if my business doesn't work out as I've planned, I can leverage my project management skills to find other opportunities.

Where is Linda's sense of purpose?
Linda's sense of purpose is straightforward and simple. She enjoys spending time with family — driving her grandchildren to school, for example. She also enjoys doing work that is recognized as having high quality and value. Her embroidery business provides her with both. The custom products she creates and sells are very well received by her clients. And she can spend more time with her family than would ever be possible in a corporate role. For Linda, this is the best of all worlds.

Food for Thought:
What would be "the best of all worlds" for you? Is there a blend of work and personal life that you'd love to have, but isn't possible for you right now? How can you make that world your reality?

PAWS IN HEAVEN

Tom McGoldrick was a math whiz in high school. He credits his teacher, who was one of the authors of the National Mathematics Exam, with his success. Tom decided that he wanted to focus on either Computer Sciences or Actuarial Sciences in college and targeted two prospective schools, Purdue and Wharton. Because Tom lived in Indiana, he chose Purdue because it was the most cost effective option. He graduated with a degree in Computer Science (testing out of engineering calculus), and thought, "What's next?" Graduate school seemed like the best next step so, one year later, Tom was awarded an M.S. in Industrial Administration. Looking back, he realizes that he has used very little of what he learned directly, but his college and graduate school experience was invaluable because it taught him how to learn and he has never stopped learning since then.

After graduation, he had six job interviews, received six offers, and he accepted the offer from American National Bank and Trust in Chicago. At that time, banks in Illinois couldn't have branches. There were a large number of small banks for which American National processed transactions. Tom worked as a systems programmer for their Service Bureau, Teledata. He was very successful, and was later elected Operations Officer of the bank. He was with American National for four years.

He then joined Knauf Fiberglass (GMBH). The Knauf family owned the company, and their second generation managed it. They provided Tom with a rare learning experience through observing their interactions and noting the differences in business perspective from the mid-management to the senior-management level.

Next, Tom joined Hobart (which at that time included Kitchen-Aid) in Troy, Ohio as a project manager. From there, he became Executive Director and Chief Administrative Officer of the Metropolitan Dayton Educational Cooperative Association (MDECA), a non-profit consortium of public school districts, where he was responsible for business consulting and I.T. services. Six years later, he joined the Standard Register Company in Dayton, Ohio, to head up their IT area. Later, he joined Clark American/Checks in the Mail, the third largest check printer in the United States, where he was responsible for their entire I.T. organization. He was appointed to the first Senior Vice President position in the history of the company, and was later a key leader in efforts that ultimately led to Clark American receiving the prestigious Malcolm Baldrige Quality Award in 2001.

He left Clark in 2002 during a downsizing/reorganization. He says, "I was very upset at the time...angry...so...I wallpapered every room in the house. After a couple of months, I was able to move on. My wife, Sue Ann, and I talked about what we wanted the rest of our life to be like. We had five children, and Sue Ann had almost single-handedly raised the four oldest children due to my corporate commitments. I didn't want to go back into the corporate world where we would be in that same situation all over again. We wanted to spend more time together, so we began talking about the possibility of having our own business. We developed a list of criteria and considered over 1200 different businesses, narrowed that down to 100, and then looked at each of these 100 against a second screening of objectives that we developed. From that effort, we found 12 candidates and began to perform due diligence on them. The first one took us a month. After we had done a few, we got smarter and could "smell" problems faster. We finally narrowed the list down to 6.

We have always been pet lovers and owners. In the past, we had thought about the possibility of breeding dogs. Our Labrador Retriever, Apollo, was from Light Brigade, which is among the best bloodlines for Labradors. After doing a lot of research we decided that, while dog breeding would be interesting and great fun, we probably couldn't make a living at it. When Apollo died, we looked for a facility that would provide him with the honor and respect in disposing of his remains that we felt he deserved. We discovered there were almost none, and knew that we were fortunate to find Paws in Heaven, owned and operated by Henry and Karen Thompson. Paws in Heaven is a pet crematory that, in addition to the crematory, provides funeral services, allowing owners to "walk through" the process with their pets, if they wish. We were very impressed with the quality of the services they provided and the care they took with the pets.

Then, in June, 2003, we learned that the Thompsons were thinking about selling Paws, as they wanted to retire. Since we had experienced Paws from the customer perspective, we understood the value that this business provides. This was something we could feel really good about doing! We also recognized the opportunity for growth. Paws in Heaven now cares for 16,000 pets per year with 8,000 to 9,000 having individual cremations.

Tom bought the business in October, 2003 using half of his 401k funds and savings for 25% of the purchase price and financing 75%. They now have 8 employees and three trucks. He is able to leverage his past experience, using his business knowledge in managing and relationship building, and using technology as a tool, with several PCs, a DSL link and QuickBooks. They work 80-hour weeks, but it is truly a labor of love.

Tom's Advice to Others

- Begin by considering your personal finances. Then think about what you can do within those limitations.

- Think about what you want and put your criteria in writing. What would you feel good about doing? What would give you a sense that you're providing value? We were fortunate to have a coach who helped guide us through this process.

- When you have identified possibilities, perform due diligence, but don't get bogged down in "analysis paralysis". After reviewing several possibilities, you will have a pretty good sense of what passes your "smell test". As our coach told us, your time is very important at this stage, and you do not want to waste much time looking at possibilities that are simply not going to work out. Rather, you need to develop the skills to eliminate situations as early as possible, so you can move on to the next opportunity. Remember, one of your objectives is to stop your "cash drain" and begin earning a living again!

- Understand the importance of direct customer contact. That's where the business comes from. Learn to build relationships. Relationships will carry you further, whether inside or outside I.T., than your technical competence can.

- Always look at the business reasons. Many I.T. people are great at building elegant solutions that don't solve a business problem or that don't add any real value to the business. A former associate once told me that a strategic objective of any business is that you first "don't do anything to jeopardize the business". Many I.T. solutions have been implemented without taking this into consideration.

This is Tom's formula for success:

Passion + Persistence = Success. Tom says, "Every successful person has fallen down a few times. Use these incidents as learning situations. Most of all, have confidence in yourself!"

What did you identify as Tom's Purpose?

Tom's passion and purpose are grounded in his family and in being of service to others. Like many of the other story-tellers, Tom recognized that his career in the corporate world, while providing his family with a comfortable lifestyle, had significantly diminished his ability to participate in family life. He also recognized that he wanted to do work that would provide more direct benefit to others. Having the experience of saying goodbye to his much-loved pet provided Tom with an unexpected opportunity. He was able to blend his love of animals, his desire to be of service to others, and his need to spend more time with his family into a new career direction that fully enacted his purpose.

Food for Thought:

Are there conflicting demands on your time? How would you prefer to be spending it?

How can you change your activities to make more time to spend with those you love, doing those things you love?

MUSIC IN THE NUMBERS AND THE WORDS

Norman Daoust is an independent computer consultant who specializes in information modeling and systems integration. And...he has a not-so-secret life: he's a musician and a speaker.

For 24 years, Norman was in corporate I.T. roles, beginning as a computer programmer, and later specializing in data modeling and healthcare data integration, with the exception of a three-year "temporary retirement" in the 1980's during which he focused on his music. Norman plays "fretted instruments": the guitar, electric bass, banjo and mandolin. For the first year, he played with a band, and later freelanced with different bands. In part because of the ups and downs in the music profession, he decided to return to the corporate world, and he was able to land a full-time job that still provided him time for his music.

After returning to the corporate environment, Norman remembered all of the things in the past that had led him to "temporarily retire". While working on a high-profile, high-pressure project, he found he was having trouble getting up to go to work in the morning. He had issues with the way the project was being managed. He thought, "This could be a lot better...I could do it better." But, as he considered this further, he realized that his issues were rooted in the inability of large bureaucratic organizations to embrace and manage change. So he began considering alternatives. He thought about consulting, and participated in several consulting workshops, but he was not yet willing to "jump off the diving board". He liked the work he was doing; he just didn't enjoy the environment. Then...he was laid off.

He says, "I thought about finding another job, but I realized that it would have to be with a large company, given the types of work I like to do. I also realized I'd probably stay with that company until I retired. Several of my good friends had become consultants over the past two years. I thought that if I didn't take the chance to become a consultant now, I never would.

A friend of mine, Andy Woyak, told me about how Andy Grove, then CEO of Intel, makes hard decisions when there are two choices. He asks himself, "When I die, which one would I regret most not having done?" When I thought about that, the answer became clear to me: I must try it! I thought: What's the worst thing that can happen? No one will hire me! If no one hires me for a year, I'll go back and look for a corporate job. I'll be no worse off than

I am now, except that I'll have less in savings. So…I became an independent consultant in 2001."

Just before he was laid off, Norman was scheduled to participate in a conference call to assist several groups that were planning a six-month part-time project with the Centers for Disease Control and Prevention — he's an expert in healthcare data exchange. After indicating that he would be leaving his current employer in three weeks and was considering consulting, they asked if he would like to work on the project as an independent consultant. Within 60 days, he had a second opportunity to work on a project with the CIHI (Canadian Institute of Health Information). His consulting career was launched!

Norman attributes his success not so much to his technical expertise but instead to his willingness to listen and to facilitate groups to work effectively together. What he enjoys most about consulting are the interesting clients and projects coupled with the challenges of continuous learning, the freedom to explore new avenues of business, and the enjoyment of public speaking.

Norman's Advice to Others:
- Learn how to run a business. There's a lot to learn. Marketing, sales, negotiating rates, sending invoices and following up on them, and so on. Oh, and you have the opportunity to do some consulting as well!
- Remember that consulting can be either "Feast or Famine". For example, I worked 65 hours a week on two different projects — one long-term, another short-term high profile, for two months. I really focus when I'm working, so I was very tired when it was over. I didn't want to work forty hour weeks for months at a stretch. My ideal schedule would be 20 to 25 hours a week. That way, I would always have enough time to learn new things and pursue other activities. But that's not the way it always works, so be prepared to be flexible with your schedule.
- Most of my consulting engagements come as a result of networking. A great networking opportunity is speaking to groups. This didn't come naturally for me…I fell into it. I was participating in a conference, and was asked to do a brief summary of my work on data exchange models for a group there. Then I was asked to coordinate a meeting of stakeholders. That brief summary turned into two half hour presentations for 100 people each and finally a fifteen minute presentation for a group of 600 people! At dinner that evening after my final presentation, Mead Walker, a colleague, said "So, Norman, you were a little nervous, eh?" Later, a good friend and fellow

consultant, Mark Campbell, told me I'd experience more benefits than I would ever imagine after I mentioned I'd been meaning to attend a Toastmasters meeting. He told me he'd been a member for years and would never be in the position he's in if it weren't for his Toastmasters experience. So I joined...3 chapters at once: Chatter by the Charles, the A.D. Little Chapter and the Humor and Drama Chapter at MIT, to learn 3 times as fast! Best of all, I learned to really enjoy public speaking. I'm now participating in the second round of a speech competition for Toastmasters International. I speak to all kinds of groups: conferences, business associations, and networking associations such as WIND (Wednesday is Networking Day), the 495 Networking Support Group, Face2Face Job Search Networking Group, the Acton Networkers Group. These are all great networking opportunities!

- Join organizations. We are not independent — we are all *interdependent* consultants. I have learned the most about consulting from other consultants. I actively participate in several consultant associations: ICCA (Independent Computer Consultants Association) and SPC (Society for Professional Consultants). I'm past president of the Boston Chapter of the ICCA.
- You really need an explicit support group — both computer consultants and those outside your field. Associations are great places to find them.
- Learn to market yourself. Think and act like a consultant while you're still employed in the corporate world. Learn how to promote yourself, how to get known, how to help others know the kind of work you do — this is a crucial skill for consultants. You need to hear the music in what you do and show that to others!

Did you hear Norman's purpose?

Norman highly values continuous learning, both for himself and others. His work is to enable change in organizations and his public speaking engagements have provided great opportunities for Norman to enact his purpose. And the music plays through everything he says and does!

Food for Thought:

What opportunities do you have to enact your purpose that you may not now be taking advantage of? What can you do to leverage those opportunities?

ROCK THE BOAT!

Victor Pontes describes himself today as a SAS programmer, and an independent consultant. That's miles away from where he was when he graduated from college with a degree in history.

Upon graduating, he discovered there were no opportunities, other than teaching, in which he could use his education. So, he took a job stuffing envelopes for a direct travel marketing company. He soon advanced from envelope-stuffing to supervising data entry temps and, in that role, interacted with the marketing programmer. He was interested in what the programmer did and wanted to learn more about it, but couldn't engage the "somewhat cantankerous" individual in any conversation. So, Victor peered over his shoulder and wrote down what he saw. The programmer was working in SQL. Victor experimented with it after hours and discovered that he could actually do the queries. When the programmer left the company, Victor, self-taught, landed the job.

He later joined ABT Associates, where he was responsible for producing financial reports. He noticed what the SAS programmer there was doing and thought, "I could do that! He knew it would be a much better opportunity financially, so he enrolled in SAS training and became a SAS programmer. He transferred from the Cambridge office to Washington, D.C., and then to Amsterdam, the Netherlands, at the height of the software industry boom. He was laid off after six months and returned to the U.S....on September 9, 2001.

He found an opportunity to use his SAS expertise at Channing Lab, the Harvard University medical research facility. He joined the SAS programmers group, and learned, from conversations with peers, that he could earn twice as much as a consultant, so he decided to go independent in 2006.

Victor's Advice to Others

- When I submitted my resignation, I had already been offered an opportunity for an engagement that would begin as two days per week and grow into five days per week. I offered my manager the opportunity of keeping me on for the other days. He took me up on my offer, and that enabled me to more easily transition to my own business. I "rocked the boat" and it worked out, but I was prepared for the worst-case scenario. I could still have managed if my manager had said, "No."

- If you don't love what you do, don't do it. Being paid to do what I love to do — that's a great motivator for me. I work a lot of hours. I worked a lot of hours in my corporate role, too. It's easier, being independent, because I'm paid by the hour. In my corporate role, I was on salary — I wasn't paid for overtime.

- I wasn't comfortable initially in marketing myself. But I learned that reputation brings opportunities. Most of my work comes through referrals from clients or other SAS programmers that I have met through the SAS programmers group. It's more important to impress this group than prospective clients. Joining this group was the best thing I ever did — I have more opportunities for work than I can take on!

- I don't enjoy the details of managing the business, but I understand how important they are. I'm lucky to have my wife acting as my business manager. She has more experience in managing a business, and that frees up my time to work more hours. We always keep in mind that things can change, and we put money away for those times when I may not be so busy.

Where is Victor's purpose?

Victor's purpose may not have been so easy to see, and that's because you may be looking too hard. Victor simply wants to be "paid for doing what I love to do", in order to build a good life for his wife and himself.

Food for Thought:

You may remember that I said at the beginning of this book that your life purpose doesn't have to be a lofty one. For many people, it isn't. But articulating it provides focus and structure for all of your life's activities. So...have you written your life purpose yet? If not, why not?

LEVERAGING THE WISDOM OF EXPERIENCE

Vin D'Amico graduated from Northeastern University with a degree in Mathematics. There were no computer science degrees then, however the Math curriculum at Northeastern included a number of computer science courses. Northeastern's co-op program provided Vin with the opportunity of working and gaining some experience in mainframe software development (then called data processing). He was able to leverage that experience later to work on government contracts for the space program.

This was the era of the large IBM mainframes. As technology continued to develop, Vin shifted his focus from mainframes to mini-computers, then to micro-controllers (computerized products) and PC's. He joined the contracting world in the early 80's, specializing in the PL/M control language.

This was a good time to be in the software industry. There were many opportunities for him to use his specialty. He landed a three-month contract with Wang Laboratories to develop printer software and actually completed the work in six weeks. Wang extended his contract and made several attempts to hire him, offering him a management position that he finally accepted. Vin stayed with Wang for eight years, although the later years were difficult ones at Wang. One morning, without any warning, a headline appeared in the Lowell Sun saying that Wang was laying off 3,000 people. Vin found himself in the unfortunate position of personally having to conduct 30 layoffs — not something he wanted to do, or ever experience again.

After Wang, Vin joined MicroTouch, a company that developed touch screen technology, as Director of Software Development. He was responsible for developing microcontroller and PC software. He was doing well, but as the company's fortune changed he decided to move on.

Vin eventually joined Keane, Inc., an I.T. software development and management consulting company. This was his first experience in business software development. He was assigned to a project with Arthur Andersen, but when the software industry took a downturn, Keane released a number of consultants. Vin once again found himself in the situation that he had experienced earlier at Wang. Seeing "the handwriting on the wall", he decided to look outside Keane for other opportunities.

Vin joined Corporate Technologies, a re-seller for SUN Microsystems UNIX products. Corporate Technologies wanted to develop software applications and sell them. Unfortunately in 2000–2001, their revenue was cut in half. Vin wondered if he should bail out. He thought he would probably have to take a huge cut in salary to stay on, so instead of looking for another corporate opportunity that might lead to the same outcome, he decided to "go out on his own", returning to contracting, this time as an independent consultant.

His first year — 2003 — was a tough one, however in 2004 he landed a couple of big contracts with EMC, and from there he was able to build a very successful consulting business, and has retained EMC as one of clients since then.

Vin's Advice to Others

- I learned a lot about what not to do from life's experiences. There were warning signs I should have heeded. Even while you are in the corporate environment, you need to treat yourself as a business, managing your career and your skills development. It helps to have a specialty that is in demand. Keep your resume updated, and develop an exit strategy — what will you do if you learn that layoffs are coming?

- Being a consultant can be challenging, but there are many resources available to help you. The Government's Small Business Association provides a wealth of information. Professional associations are also great. For example, I belong to the Institute of Management Consultants. They offer good educational opportunities and mentoring. In retrospect, I wish I had found a mentor earlier in my career.

- Running your own business is hard. You wear a lot of hats. You're "Chief of Everything" — sales, marketing, business management. You can either do it all yourself or hire others to do it for you. Hiring others can make a lot of sense, because running a business truly is harder than it looks.

- You need to develop good marketing skills. Networking doesn't come naturally for many in I.T., however making contacts are essential to your success as a consultant. You need a good, high-quality website. Using postcard campaigns to reach buyers can be very effective — there are several companies that you can hire to do these. You can also get your name out there by publishing articles. I have a monthly column in the Indus Business Journal.

- When you're deciding whether or not to "go it on your own", it's important to stick to the facts, and not let your emotions guide you in decision-making. You need some money to fall back on initially.

If the situation you're considering doesn't make good financial sense for you, don't go there. Starting a new business is about risk-taking. If you have the experience and can afford to take the risk, then go for it.

Does Vin have a purpose?

The answer is "yes", but once again it may be a bit difficult to see. Vin loves the variety, the challenges, and the opportunities for continuous learning that consulting provides him. As a result, he is able to share the wisdom of his experience with others.

Food for Thought:

So...what do you want to do with the rest of your life? Remember that those things you choose will define who you are.

WHAT'S NEXT? — MAKING PLANS FOR YOUR FUTURE

Now that you've heard these stories, are you ready to take the next step? Here are some thoughts that can help you create the future of your dreams!

Use The Law of Attraction

So many people don't have any idea of what they want for their future. Remember this old saying: If you don't know where you're going, any road will take you there?" You can get somewhere, but is it really somewhere you want to be?

Here's a tip — you create the future. Really! Everything you're doing today is setting the stage for your future.

Here's how it works. If the people around you see that you're taking the initiative to develop yourself, and they know what opportunities you're looking for, they'll keep their eyes and ears open for you. If they find an opportunity that fits, they'll tell you about it. Following through on these tips, you'll very likely land an opportunity that moves you to the next step in your career. So, through your actions, you're shaping your future.

There's a popular book and video today called The Secret. It's about a theory called the Law of Attraction. One description of it says that "thoughts become things". Thoughts have energy, they go out into the universe through your actions, and "like" attracts "like". If your thoughts are positive, your actions will be positive and you'll attract positive results. If your thoughts are negative, your actions will be negative and you'll attract negative results.

Daydream Your Perfect Day

To design your future, you first need to think about what you'd like that future to be. Many only think about what they don't want the future to be. Push those negative thoughts aside. Sit back, put your feet up, play some relaxing music, close your eyes, and envision a perfect day in your future. Where are you? What do you see? What do you hear? What do you feel? Who else is there with you? What are you doing? Now that you're there, on your perfect day, keep going. Your perfect day is a "moving picture". Imagine you're creating a video of your perfect day — beginning, middle and end. Now, roll footage!

Plan Your Future — Backward and Forward

Once your Perfect Day is clear in your mind, you're ready to figure out how you can turn it into your future reality. What things would you need to have in place to create that day? How would you go about getting those things you need? What would you need to do to prepare to get them? And so on. Borrowing from Stephen Covey, "Begin with the end in mind", work backward step by step, noting each step (input — process — output) until you arrive at where you are today. Now, turn the process around. You have just created a plan for achieving your dream future!

Call to Action

So many people live in a state of regret. They regret that they didn't choose a different direction earlier in their lives and they beat themselves up over it regularly. Instead of focusing on "What's next?" they spend many hours asking themselves, "What if?" They can't accept the idea that it isn't too late for them to do something different. Their regret disables them.

There are also people who welcome every morning, who live every day to the fullest, who breathe hope and anticipation into everything they do.

I invite you now to take the first step to assure that the rest of your life is the best of your life!

APPENDIX

COMPETENCIES THAT ENABLE A SUCCESSFUL CAREER

D rawing from the great advice these story-tellers have given, here are the competencies that enabled their success and can help you to assure your own!

Work/Life Competencies

Vision
- Look at economics, trends, become a futurist.
- Understand where you want to go in your life.
- Think about what you want and put it in writing.
- Figure out what you really want to do, and do it — don't just follow the money.

Networking/Connecting with Others
- Learn to build relationships. Relationships will carry you further than your technical competence can.
- Learn how to promote yourself, how to get known, how to help others know the kind of work you do.
- Develop speaking skills. Many business relationships come from speaking to associations and other groups.
- The people you meet can provide assistance and opportunities.
- They can become an extended support group, in addition to your family and friends.

Customer/Relationship Satisfaction
- Customer/relationship satisfaction is critical to your success.
- Understand the importance of direct contact.
- Stay tuned to what your customers want, what they like about you and what they don't.
- Your customers are your best source of advertising.

Mentoring
- Get a mentor in your field whom you can respect, and let him or her help you from the beginning.
- Become a sponge; ask questions.
- Following someone else's model for success is the quickest way to developing your own.

Self-Development
- Continually re-invent and improve yourself.
- Inventory those things you have done that represent success to you.
- Ask yourself what led to your taking these actions.
- Review your actions for patterns.
- Choose to do those things that fit the patterns, those things you have an affinity or liking for.

Business Savvy
- Research what you're drawn to.
- Carefully study every aspect of the business you're interested in.
- Do the analysis, understand the business and what you're committing to.
- Recognize and take advantage of opportunities when they come.
- Always look at the business reasons.
- Understand that it's a business.
- Be a "realistic optimist".

Financial Management
- If you don't have the skills, hire someone who can do it for you.
- Don't underestimate your expenses.
- Do understand the level of risk you're willing to take.

Passion/Purpose
- Find and do what you love. Discover what makes you happy, satisfied, content, even if others may consider it to be "off the wall".
- Find a purpose, love in your life; think about what really matters to you.
- Enthusiasm is important. Find your passion and pursue it.
- Be passionate about what you do - make your passion your business.

Persistence
- Determine and implement actions to achieve your goals.
- Passion plus persistence equals success.

Confidence
- Take control of your life.
- Believe in yourself.
- Trust your competence.
- Reputation is competence plus confidence.

Flexibility/Adaptability
- Don't allow yourself to be "stuck in a box."
- Find opportunities to try out your chosen role.
- Draw on what you know.
- Be flexible with your schedule.

Resiliency
- Allow yourself to make mistakes.
- Learn from your mistakes and go on.
- Develop strategies to deal with stress.
- Make time to relax and enjoy that time.
- Don't get discouraged — just do it!

ON THE BRINK OF DISASTER?

D o you ever feel like you're on the brink of financial disaster? Are you thinking, "Well…I did, but everything is okay now!" Remember the old adage: History repeats itself? And another one: Those who fail to learn from the past are doomed to repeat it? Many of us have been lulled into a false sense of security. Many, but not all. There's Senator Byron L. Dorgan, North Dakota, who has served for 25 years in the U. S. Congress. He spent twelve years in the U.S. House of Representatives serving on the powerful Ways and Means Committee, and three terms in the U.S. Senate. He has become one of America's leading voices calling for a change in the economic and trade policies that have resulted in shipping American jobs overseas, undercutting our farmers and workers, and creating a mountain of trade debt that threatens our country's future. Here's an excerpt of what he has to say about where we're going in his book, "Take This Job And Ship It!: How Corporate Greed and Brain-Dead Politics Are Selling Out America" (2006).

Even the rosiest predictions, suggest that, if this (trend) continues, America will lose 10 percent of its manufacturing jobs and millions more white-collar jobs in the next decade to cheap overseas labor…

Think back. Most typical Americans probably came from a family in which the father worked while the mother stayed home with the children. You probably enjoyed a good standard of living, had plenty to eat, and your parents had enough time to raise you right.

Now look at your life. You've got two cars. The kids are in day care. Both spouses work. And work longer hours. On your block there are smaller families and bigger houses. The mortgage is a backbreaker. The credit cards are maxed out. Your employer can no longer afford Blue Cross, so you have to pay for your own health insurance, too. And that defined-benefit pension plan you used to have? Forget it! What happened to the American family? How did we lose ground? And why? Some of it is born of our own materialism.

Many of us, living in "the land of plenty", are finding ourselves constrained by "golden handcuffs". With inexpensive goods so readily available, we have become "stuff junkies". You may remember that the comedian George Carlin had a routine he performed about "stuff". He said that we keep acquiring more and more stuff, and then we have to buy a bigger house to hold all the stuff, and the cycle goes on and on. While his skit is very funny, it is also, sadly, very true. The trouble is, many of us are in over our heads, acquiring all that stuff on credit and paying for it with future earnings, so when we find ourselves out of a job, that lifestyle quickly becomes a disaster.

Doesn't it make sense to plan for the possibility that we may not always have the jobs we have now? Here are suggestions from the experts for some simple steps you might take to begin to break free of the golden handcuffs.

Step #1 — Write down what you spend. Most of us don't really know where our money really goes. You can't effectively manage what you don't measure.

Step #2 — Pay off your credit cards every month. If you can't pay them off, review your spending to figure out why and develop a plan to assure that you can. The interest on credit card debt is outrageous. If you carry over a balance, you'll soon find yourself paying interest on top of interest. And if you miss a payment, the rate goes up! Soon, all of the "stuff" you bought that seemed so inexpensive — well, you get the picture.

Step #3 — Most of us are in the habit of taking several vacations each year. Instead of traveling for both vacations, take one vacation away and the other at home. Take some day trips and save the airfare and hotel bills.

Step #4 — Defer buying a new vehicle for a few years after the one you have now is paid off. Put the "car payment money" into an account in the event you need to pay for any repairs beyond maintenance. In most cases, you'll come out way ahead. And the money you save can be used for a new (or used) car when you need one. (Of course, the best used car is the one you know everything about — the car you already have!)

Step #5 — Recycle the stuff inside your home. Instead of buying new furniture and accessories, repurpose and rearrange the pieces you have. Figure out what you really use. Separate the stuff you really use from the stuff you don't. Donate the stuff you don't use to charity. (Okay...some stuff does have an aesthetic quality that might not be described as "useful", and it contributes to your sense of well-being, making your space your own. You should be the judge of what's "useful" to you.)

Step #6 — Learn how to do some simple home repairs yourself. Hiring plumbers, painters and carpenters is costly.

Step #7 — Limit outside entertainment. If you're accustomed to going out to dinner and a movie, or to a concert, or to a sporting event every week, make that every other week instead.

Step #8 — If you're in a cold climate, reduce your heat thermostat setting by a few degrees during the winter months, or if you're in a warm climate, increase your air conditioning thermostat setting by a few degrees during the summer months. And use energy-efficient light bulbs. Doing these simple things can make a significant difference in your energy bills.

Step #9 — Do the yard work yourself — think about it as a part of your workout routine.

Step #10 — As you realize savings from the suggestions above, put that money into a separate savings account. If you're not in the habit of saving, an easy way to begin is by simply throwing your change into a container each night. Silly as it sounds, it really does add up quickly.

Some people have saved thousands of dollars a year by taking these steps, and in the process of saving, they have also found greater peace of mind.

RESOURCES

Books
It's Only Too Late If You Don't Start Now by Barbara Sher
What Color is Your Parachute? by Richard Nelson Bolles
Working Identity by Herminia Ibarra
Losing Your Job, Reclaiming Your Soul by Mary Lynn Pulley
We Are All Self-Employed by Cliff Hakim
Do What You Love, The Money Will Follow by Marsha Sinetar
Thriving in Transition by Marcia Perkins-Reed
Leaving Microsoft to Change the World by John Wood
The Law of Attraction by Michael Losier
The Secret by Rhonda Byrne

Organizations

The Small Business Administration
www.sba.gov (from their website)

Over the past 47 years, SBA has grown in terms of total assistance provided and its array of programs tailored to encourage small enterprises in all areas. SBA's programs now include financial and federal contract procurement assistance, management assistance, and specialized outreach to women, minorities and armed forces veterans. The SBA also provides loans to victims of natural disasters and specialized advice and assistance in international trade.

Nearly 20 million small businesses have received direct or indirect help from one or another of those SBA programs since 1953, as the agency has become the government's most cost-effective instrument for economic development. In fact, SBA's current business loan portfolio of roughly 219,000 loans worth more than $45 billion makes it the largest single financial backer of U.S. businesses in the nation.

Over the past 10 years, (FY 1991-2000), the SBA has helped almost 435,000 small businesses get more than $94.6 billion in loans, more than in the entire history of the agency before 1991. No other lender in this country — perhaps no other lender in the world — has been responsible for as much small business financing as the SBA has during that time.

Since 1958, SBA's venture capital program has put more than $30 billion into the hands of small business owners to finance their growth.

Last year alone, the SBA backed more than $12.3 billion in loans to small businesses. More than $1 billion was made available for disaster loans and more than $40 billion in federal contracts were secured by small businesses with SBA's help.

SBA continues to branch out to increase business participation by women and minorities along new avenues such as the minority small business program, microloans and the publication of Spanish language informational materials.

There are those who argue that big businesses, profiting from "economies of scale," can produce far more efficiently than small businesses. But small business is where the innovations take place. Swifter, more flexible and often more daring than big businesses, small firms produce the items that line the shelves of America's museums, shops and homes. They keep intact the heritage of ingenuity and enterprise and they help keep the "American Dream" within the reach of millions of Americans. Every step of the way, SBA is there to help them.

SCORE (Counselors to America's Small Business)
www.score.org (from their website)

SCORE "Counselors to America's Small Business" is America's premier source of free and confidential small business advice for entrepreneurs. Get biz advice today.
- Resource partner with the U.S. Small Business Administration
- Headquartered in Herndon, Virginia and Washington, D.C
- SCORE is a 501 (c) (3) nonprofit organization dedicated to the formation, growth and success of small businesses nationwide
- Formed in 1964, SCORE provides a public service to America by offering small business advice and training

SCORE Has Helped More Than 7.5 Million Small Businesses
We've helped Vermont Teddy Bear, Vera Bradley Designs, Jelly Belly Candy. More successes.

Live Your Dream SCORE Can Help
SCORE offers <u>Ask SCORE email advice online</u>.

Independent Computer Consultants Association

www.icca.org (from their website)

The Independent Computer Consultants Association (ICCA) represents a wide variety of information technology consultants who provide consulting, implementation, support, training, strategic planning, and business analysis services. Our member firms are independent, i.e., they will only propose to do work that is within their core competence, and will not be unduly influenced by any vendor or product.

The ICCA, established in 1976 and headquartered in St. Louis, MO, is a not-for-profit trade organization whose primary purpose is to elevate the quality of the computer consulting industry. Our member firms believe that ethical conduct, excellent work product, and honest dealing with their clients are the way to succeed in business. Our member firms strive to implement elegant solutions that fulfill their client's need while meeting the dual constraints time and money. ICCA helps its member firms by providing member benefits, services, and local chapters in metropolitan areas where like-minded consultants can meet and learn from each other.

Joanne Dustin is a career/life transition coach, an executive coach and an organizational development consultant with over 25 years' experience in the I.T. industry focused on leadership development, career development, organizational change management, and talent management.

Joanne is the founder and principal of three coaching/consulting practices:

Career Lost and Found
(www.careerlostandfound.com)
- guiding professionals through career/life transitions to a future in which they are fully engaged, living and working with passion and purpose

Changing Retirement
(www.changingretirement.com)
- enabling organizations and individuals to design and implement dynamic and innovative retirement strategies

Synergy Consulting Collaborative
(www.synergyconsultingcollaborative.com)
- an association of independent consultants, focused on strengthening organizational effectiveness through employee engagement

Joanne has been a featured speaker at conferences and professional associations, and has authored many articles on career/life changes and employee engagement.

She is a Professional Certified Career Coach, Career Coach Institute, a Certified Coach of Leaders, Linkage, Inc., and a member of the International Association of Career Coaches, the Association of Career Professionals International, the International Coach Federation, the Northeast Human Resources Association, Women in Technology International, and the National Association of Female Executives.

Joanne holds an MS in Organization and Management from Antioch University — New England, and a BS in Management and Computer Science from Franklin Pierce University.

Life Beyond I.T.: Open the Door…Your Future is Waiting, is her first book.

3384014

Made in the USA